FRONTP
HISTORY

RESEARCHING AND TELLING YOUR FAMILY'S STORIES

BY TAMMY MARSHALL CARDWELL

FORWARD BY ROB SHEARER

Dedicated to...

Granny and Grandaddy, who always believed.

Acknowledgments

This book owes its existence, and I owe my thanks, to a great many people...

Dawn, for suggesting I write it in the first place...

Jack, Thomas and Terry, for living with me while I did...

Cindy and Judy, for proofing endless drafts and improving
my grammar skills in the process...

Peggy, for pushing me in Rob's direction & Rob, for putting up with the nut from Texas...

Mr. Dickson, for showing us all that history is more than names and dates...

And, most important, God, for making me able.

Published by
Greenleaf Books, LLC
3761 Highway 109N, Unit D, Lebanon, TN 37087
First Edition
March 1999

Internet: www.greenleafpress.com
3761 Highway 109 N., Unit D
Lebanon, TN 37087
615-449-1617

Greenleaf
P · R · E · S · S

Table of Contents

Forward

Family and history — two of my favorite topics! Modern man has been busy trying to disfigure and dismantle both of them, which just shows how important it is to preserve them and pay attention to them.

As I have reached middle age, I've discovered a new and deeper interest in my family. And, much to my surprise, I've discovered my children are already interested in what their grandparents and great-grandparents were like — they're not waiting till they reach middle age. My own arrested development in this area must have something to do with being a child of the 1950's & 1960's when the family was dismissed as hopelessly outmoded, and "bourgeoisie."

After our own family had swelled to ten children, I discovered that my own grandfather had been the youngest of ten children. Now, I'm sure my mother must have mentioned this to me as I was growing up, but I had no "ears to hear." The more I looked into the matter, the more interesting it became. We have all sorts of unusual figures in the family tree: A Hugenot family who came to South Carolina in the 1700's; A Virginia judge who served in the colonial legislature along with Patrick Henry; a Virginia colonist who was given a 6,000 acre tract in the colony of Virginia which later turned into the cities of Norfolk and Virginia Beach (and if I found out which of my ancestors sold the land… Well!); and (if one of my genealogically minded cousins is to be believed) a line of descent which goes all the way back to Robert the Bruce, King of Scotland.

My oldest son particularly liked finding out the last little tidbit. It got him started on kilts, claymores, bagpipes, Grandfather Mountain, celtic games… and what looks now like it might be a career as a celtic musician. It also gave us some wonderful opportunities to talk about our family and about what's important.

We've also gotten a chance to talk about the experiences of our immediate family and how they were affected by the great events of the last 200 years. My great-grandfather was a surgeon with Robert E. Lee's Army of Northern Virginia. My grandfather worked in Panama on the canal along with Dr. Walter Reed, then came back to Georgia as State Director of Public Health — the Atlanta newspapers credited him with eliminating malaria from the state of Georgia. My father (who died when I was young) graduated from West Point in 1941 and wound up serving in Europe with General Patton, and after the war in Japan with MacArthur. My stepfather was on detached service with Chiang Kai Shek's soldiers in China during WW II. Just before he died, we looked at an Atlas of China together to see how many of the cities he had been in, I had been able to visit when we adopted our daughter from China in 1997.

All of these are more than just bits of historical trivia. They help us to understand our family, ourselves, their times and our times as well. And when we talk about these things with our own children, they are much richer for understanding the connections between generations and the circumstances that shaped, however indirectly, their own lives.

Our culture has made a fetish of living for the moment. We pretend the past doesn't matter… doesn't affect us. But it does, even when we adamantly deny it. It is not just better to understand the past — our own past — than to be shaped by it without understanding it. It is actually a part of the biblical pattern for family life. The "things" which fathers are to teach their children from Deuteronomy are actually family stories, front-porch history from ancient Israel.

Tammy Cardwell has done a wonderful job of reminding us how important both history and family are. She has given us not just a wonderful collection of practical how-to suggestions, she has reminded us of the reasons why we should undertake the task. Front Porch History is real history. All of us, and especially our children, will be richer for reading Tammy's book, and embarking on the adventure she recommends.

I'm glad she has reminded me of the importance of my own family history. I commend her book to the gentle community of readers and families everywhere.

— Rob Shearer
Greenleaf Press
March 31st, 1999

Chapter 1

Family Stories?

For generations, family history passed from parent to child to grandchild through stories. Stories were told by the fire in the evening, to children snuggled in warmed winter beds, on the front porches of summer as day slowly gave way to night… Stories were told wherever the storyteller found an eager listener, and there were always eager listeners.

Tradition, and the passing on of heritage through family stories, was a vital part of days long gone, days when FAMILY was a word highly honored, and when honor was generally understood. These were days when we, as a people, had a self-respect that is no longer common, when courtesy was the standard, and when crime was the exception rather than the rule.

We've heard theory upon theory regarding our degradation as a people, and there seems to be some truth in most of the theories. I personally feel that the failure is within each individual and that the individual fails, in part, because he has been failed. In spite of all that he has been given, all that he has learned, he lacks something vital — personal heritage.

Time, you see, has become a "four-letter word," one used in exclamations of frustration. Families can't find any time to spend together, and certainly not for such a 'trivial' pursuit as recounting the adventures of relatives long gone. When time does not hold us back, 'truth' puts forth its exacting demands. Heaven forbid that we should tell our children an untruth, and everyone knows that half of all family stories are heavily embellished, so out go half of the stories. Add to all of this the fact that the mere thought of telling stories makes us uncomfortable and you see how easy it is to excuse never making the attempt.

I was fortunate. I had a grandfather who enjoyed introducing children to their ancestors. It was not at all uncommon to see a child at Grandaddy's feet, soaking up tales of ancestors who would otherwise have been nothing more than sepia-toned images in a faded photo album. Through Grandaddy's stories we became intimately familiar with those who had gone before us. We learned of people who were well-meaning but imperfect, men and women who worked eagerly to fulfill their dreams, and brave individuals who had the courage to step out into the unknown. Grandaddy's stories gave us the opportunity to see life from a different perspective while also providing an anchor, a sense of who we were and where we'd come from. They illustrated over and over again that normal people, individuals like ourselves, were capable of living lives worth remembering. Also, although I don't think Grandaddy knew it, he gave us examples to follow. Within his stories, were some of the most positively effective role models of all.

Most people realize that those who read quality literature tend to acquire many of the characters' positive traits and learn to recognize negative attributes as well. The reader often uses elements of the story as a tool to judge and improve himself. Family stories can accomplish much the same thing. The child who grows up admiring Uncle Fred will naturally work to strengthen the admired qualities in his own life. The natural instinct to emulate a role model is satisfied by a model who is remembered fondly, and is a member of the family — one who belongs to the listener. In a world where the common role models are two-dimensional images on a television screen, this is an aspect of sharing family tales that is well worth considering.

Think on this. If a family of children grows up admiring and emulating worthy relatives and ancestors, that family is more likely to produce a generation deserving of praise. Likewise, if a city full of children were to grow up in such a manner, that generation would be more likely to prove a benefit to the community. And, if a nation of children...

To expect to so influence a nation of children would be unrealistic. A city full of children would also be more than one person could hope to reach. We all have the power to touch our own children, however, and these are the ones to whom we owe a debt — the stories that reveal who they are and where they came from.

In all of this, I've touched only one reason for passing on your family's stories. There are many more, some obvious and others not; the benefits are so varied and far reaching that I cannot claim to know them all. It should be obvious that bonds grow stronger when family members gather for such a time of sharing. Not only are you truly interacting with one another, but the stories offer common ground to build on, common events to reminisce about, and common heroes. Children also experience their culture through the stories, learning about it in a way that is rich and personal. They gain a pride in their heritage that cannot be found as readily elsewhere.

My own search for my family's past was inspired by these reasons and others. My husband, Jack, and I homeschool our two sons and that makes me acutely aware of my responsibilities. In the years before homeschooling, I was an expert at tossing off quick answers. Now, when my youngest asks one of his 18,532 questions, I use those questions to help him truly understand the world around him. I recognize that my responsibility toward my children extends beyond teaching them the Three R's. My goal is to also instill in them a sense of self-worth, self-confidence, and the courage to "boldly go where no man has gone before." As parents we share the responsibility of passing on our heritage, but we've grown to rely so heavily upon the schools' teaching our children "everything they (supposedly) need to know," that we forget the things they can't possibly teach — things like family.

Watching my sons, I remembered the hours spent listening to Grandaddy tell his tales and was saddened that he was not here for them today. I knew there had been something about sitting at Grandaddy's feet that made a tremendous impact on me. These were my people he was telling me about, my family pets who performed such humorous and heroic feats, my stories. I had something special and felt I was something special because of a loving old man who believed in the worth of a tale well told.

At my grandfather's death, I lost a very real connection with the past. Through the years I have forgotten all but a very few of the stories he told me and my memories of those may be inaccurate, but the effects of my time spent with him remain. I may not be the most self-confident person in the world, but Grandaddy gave me a good foundation to build on. In his stories I found that sense of who I was and who I could be. I also came to more greatly appreciate my relatives because of all we shared. The building of family spirit may be one of the most important things Grandaddy accomplished. Those of us who share this family bond are a pillar and support for each other in the hard times and are quick to rejoice with each other in the good times.

While I had grandparents who told me stories, my own children had no one. My parents both worked full-time and didn't have the freedom to sit for hours in a rocking chair talking about the past. I should have realized this, should have thought, but didn't. I, who certainly ought to have known better, was so busy educating my sons in school-related topics that I had forgotten one of the most important areas of all. I finally realized that if they were to hear any stories, it was up to me to do the telling. Having no experience with telling stories, I chose instead to write them down. I pulled out paper and pen and thought back to my childhood. Those first words were somewhat difficult, but having begun, I found that a song, or a book, or just the hum of an electric fan could trigger a flood of memories vying with each other for attention. These memories came back so alive that many were complete with tastes and smells, excitement and fear. I did write about important things that happened to me, but mostly I wrote about things that might have happened on any normal day. I especially tried to remember things I had done as a child that my sons may never have opportunity to do. Through my writing them down, recording them on paper, my boys would share at least this much of the experience.

As I did this I thought of other things I wanted them to know, things I had little or no memory of, and I asked others to help by giving me their stories. Very few obliged in the beginning, either because they felt they had nothing to tell, or they did not feel comfortable telling it. My grandmother finally shared a little about her childhood, and she ended the letter by saying, "I'm sure it won't mean to you what memory does for me." She had no way of knowing what that letter would mean to me. It was only a few months later that she left to join Grandaddy in heaven and I found myself asking, "Why didn't I start sooner? How much have I lost?"

Collecting the stories became very important to me when I realized that persons I'd been expecting to live forever could leave this earth tomorrow, taking all of their precious memories with them. This spurred my own writing and my determination to work with others. As a result, my story collection grew from a few pages to a small book that I hand-published and gave to my family. I could not bear the thought of limiting the stories to my own children when so many others may never have heard the tales.

Yes, I believe a child needs history — not just the story of the big world around him, but his story, the story of his own little world. These stories, these priceless pieces of history, slip away all too easily. We forfeit much by letting ourselves lose touch with yesterday and with each other. I have written this book in hopes of helping other families recover at least a part of that which we have lost.

Chapter 2

Where Do I Start?

You start with yourself. Your stories are as valid and important as any other, and mean far more than you know. Begin today. Share with your children the excitement of your first trip to the theater. Tell them what it felt like for the city girl to bury her toes in warm beach sand. Help them understand why your spirits rise when the distinctive scents of autumn tickle your nose.

I say, "tell the stories," and this is truly what I mean. The written word is important and I will offer suggestions for using it. I will also explain in detail how I created my family book. Do not think, however, that the written word can substitute for the spoken — it cannot. There is no substitute for the time spent together, even if you spend it debating two different people's perceptions of an event. Remember too that children have tales to tell. Treat their stories with respect, cherishing and nurturing the child's natural desire to share parts of his life with others. What we parents must relearn, our children need never forget — the joy of telling the tale.

You will not want to stop with your own stories, of course, and you shouldn't. The broader your focus, the more complete the picture becomes. Knowing this, you will find yourself seeking further, searching out other memories for you and your family to experience together. You will want to give as well, trading your own stories for those of friends and relatives. There are many ways to do this.

One option for passing along family stories is to integrate story-telling sessions into family gatherings. What better tradition to add to your list of holiday 'must do's' than that of coming together to trade tales of yesterday? You might encourage the stories by pulling out photographs and souvenirs, or by serving dishes that have memories attached. If you record the tale-telling sessions, you may even wish to begin the second gathering by playing tapes of the first. It may be difficult to get the stories started, to break through the initial uncertainty. Share a story or two of your own first and once you've begun, when everyone knows what you want, others should begin to share. The most troublesome obstacle you will have to overcome, both in yourself and in others, is the preconceived idea that you have nothing to say. In truth, my favorite among Grandaddy's stories were not those of heroic deeds or exciting adventures. I preferred the tales that presented a different picture of a person I had always known, or those that introduced me to someone I'd never had a chance to meet.

A family newsletter is another option. My children and I produce one. Through this we keep everyone abreast of family happenings and pass on one another's stories. We came about it backwards, so to speak, in that I had already compiled a family book before it occurred to me that a newsletter would be an excellent way to keep the stories coming. You could begin with the newsletter and gather the stories as you go, waiting to print them in book format later. A simple family newsletter with basic formatting could be handwritten or produced on a typewriter. We do ours on the computer, allowing my sons to develop important computer skills while they also practice writing, editing, layout and design, and more. Members of our extended family offer stories and other items of interest, and we add our own bits and pieces as we please. These bits might include news about happenings in our extended family, reviews of books and movies we've read lately, and editorials sharing where we stand on certain issues. You never know what may pop up when a family gets together, even on paper.

You may also wish to do what I did, to collect your family's stories and publish them so they will never be lost again. Perhaps you see the value of creating an heirloom to hand down from generation to generation so that those who come after will have opportunity to know you and yours. This is perhaps the most involved of all your options. Consequently, I will devote most of these pages to explaining how I compiled my own family book. It is my hope that in doing so I will make it clear that, though complex, this is not so difficult a task as it seems, and the rewards are tremendous.

Should you choose to compile a family book, you must first decide what to include, but remember to remain flexible. When I began my book it was strictly for the benefit of my own children and I planned for half a dozen copies at most. It was only after several weeks that I realized how much more exciting it would be if the whole family participated. Here is another point. When I say the whole family, I refer to my mother's side of the family. In my maternal grandmother and her six children I felt I had enough people to draw from that I could present a respectable book. It was also my mother's family that played the largest and most important parts in my childhood — and it was, after all, my childhood that I started with.

Consider carefully just how much effort you wish to put into your book, bearing in mind the amount of time you have to invest. If no one helps by sending stories, you will have to get them all yourself. This inevitably involves a great deal of time spent in one-on-one interviews and transcribing the results of those interviews.

You also want your book to be as balanced as possible, containing items of interest to all who read it. By this I mean that if you decide to include both of your parents' families in one book, and find yourself with only one or two stories representing your mother's side, the book may not be quite as interesting to her relatives. This is fine if you do not intend for her relatives to see the book, but if you want them to feel a part of it, two stories are likely not enough.

Along with the all-important issue of whom you will look to for submissions, you will also determine what type of submissions you desire. I tend to use the word stories (or tales) but there is truly little predicting what types of things you will receive. My book includes traditional (factual) stories, letters, and even a poem. My grandfather also told wonderful fictional stories, and I would have been more than happy to include some had any of us remembered them. I had decided that my family contains a wide variety of people and I wanted to represent that variety as much as possible, so I rejected nothing. One thing I especially wish my book had more of is what I call written portraits. It contains only two, and those two are incomplete, but they give the reader a very clear picture of David Marion Tisdale — the man who started it all.

I did not limit submissions — not in form, length, or subject matter. In fact, I can think of several things I would have included gladly had I received them. I would have enjoyed a section on funny things the family's children have said, or their well-reasoned (even if entirely wrong) explanations of why things are the way they are. It might be interesting to include a list of occupations family members have pursued. It comes to mind that Grandaddy and two of my uncles helped build the Baytown-La Porte tunnel, which was for decades the most convenient way to get from here to there (I live in Baytown). My Uncle Thurman was the first to drive through it, actually. He did this before they had finished, driving on wood that was lying on the floor. He drove through partly because he didn't want to take the long way home and partly because they said it couldn't be done. This is not a big story, but it is significant — especially considering this same tunnel is now a thing of the past. It was shut down not long ago, replaced by the longest cable-stayed suspension bridge in the country. In writing this book, I find myself regretting that my family book is finished and we left so much out.

I must offer some words of caution before I go any further. Your purpose in gathering your family tales should be to build family unity, not damage it. Bearing this is mind, you must realize that some embarrassing stories, and those that would hurt family members, are best left unpublished. Save this type of story for a generation or so until there is no one left to be hurt by the telling. I also advise that you not be overzealous. Do not allow this project to become a battle ground or "bone of contention," because it will then hinder the very thing you are trying to accomplish.

Regarding grammar, I chose to make only those corrections that were absolutely necessary or requested by the author. This could have been a tough decision in my grandmother's case, as her offerings were in letters and she followed her own rules of grammar. However, I feel a person's work, especially a letter, should be as that person wanted it to be. All I did to Granny's letters was include a period or two where it was obvious that she had intended they go; doing more would have made me uncomfortable. I have been proven right in this decision. She died before the book was complete and everyone who reads it appreciates the fact that her letters reflect the manner in which she spoke. Had I made extensive corrections, they would no longer have been her letters.

I will point out here that one thing I would have restricted in my family book, had it been necessary, is unacceptable language or innuendo. Remember that this is your book. You have the right to set the standards that suit you.

Chapter 3

How Do I Get the Stories?

You ask, bug, badger, cajole and interview your relatives and family friends. I include family friends because it is often they who will have some of the best stories about your family. The first step is to get on the phone and share your idea. It helps to begin by approaching those who are the type to take an idea and run with it. One of my aunts got so excited about our book that she wrote pages and pages about her childhood, assisted another aunt with her contributions, dug out a story my cousin had written for a college English class, proofed endless copies of the manuscript, and donated money to help cover expenses. During the year I worked on the book, she was a constant encouragement and invaluable assistant.

One-on-one interviews can be especially productive if you have time to invest in them. I learned this as a freshman in high school when my American History teacher instructed us to interview someone who had lived through the Depression. When my father's parents agreed to be interviewed, I prepared a list of questions — knowing I wouldn't remember even one if I didn't have them written down — and purchased a blank tape for my cassette recorder.

Once I got over my nervousness as a first-time interviewer, and they had grown accustomed to the presence of the tape player (I did ask permission before turning it on, and suggest you always do the same.), the evening became one filled with fascination. I had two people in front of me who had been children during the Depression — at nearly opposite ends of the economic spectrum. Talk about an eye-opening interview! Their lives had both been filled with love and family, but the challenges each family had faced had been worlds apart. The pleasure of that evening spent with them, and my unending fascination in the things I'd learned, may well have a lot to do with why learning more is so important to me today. It was certainly my first experience with a history that was alive and engaging!

Family reunions are perhaps one of the best places to find stories. Go armed with a tape recorder or camcorder and plenty of blank tapes and batteries. Have a list of questions prepared, as I did for my grandparents' interview, just in case. Talk enough to get the stories started then sit back and enjoy yourself. Feel free to ask questions to help keep the stories coming, but do not attempt to dictate the paths the tales take. You will find that one memory often leads to another, either for the original speaker or another member of the group. The fun really starts when three people all offer different versions of the same event. It doesn't necessarily matter which is true; they all have a place in the family collection.

Clearly identify the speaker, either on the tape or in your notes. Afterwards, transcribe the tapes as quickly as possible. By transcribing them immediately, you have a much better chance of remembering the things that happened around you while Aunt LaNelle was talking. Did Uncle Douglas get so red in the face that it led you to believe he might have been the one who hid the pig in the church? It's worth finding out, but if you wait too long you may forget this little detail. After transcribing the tapes, do not erase or misplace them. Preserve these tapes as the valuable recordings they are. Years ago, two different people recorded Grandaddy telling his stories. Both of these recordings have since disappeared, and our family considers this a tragic loss.

Listen for clues that lead to other potential storytellers. "Your Uncle Irvin spent much more time with Papa than I did He could tell you all sorts of things." "Well, I don't remember much about it, but Sophie Middleton threatened to write the whole episode up for a magazine once." This type of comment will lead you to new prospects and you should be quick to contact them. Get in touch even if they live far away. Once they realize what you want, many of these people will gladly meet with you or record their memories on tape or in writing. If there are no family reunions or holidays imminent, try a family dinner. Invite a group of relatives who interact well together, and make them comfortable around your dinner table. Serve any dishes that you know have special memories attached. You might also have your guests bring photos, souvenirs, and letters that will trigger memories long forgotten.

There are two especially important things to remember when interviewing your friends and family. Ask questions that require complete answers rather than yes/no questions, and be courteous at all times. Accept the fact that there are some things you may never learn; never pry if someone refuses to discuss a given topic. Also, be ready to stop the interview if an older participant tires or tries to push himself too hard.

When I decided to include my whole family, I sat down and wrote letters to all of those for whom I had addresses. I wrote individual letters, but a photocopied family letter might have done as well. I shared my vision and asked for their assistance, assuring them that I didn't want anything in particular and would give no prizes for professional writing. I made it clear that I wanted only to gather as much as I could of my family's past.

Maybe the letter was the best place to start, but it received little response. I think that, next time, I will budget instead for a few long distance phone calls. Not only are people today so busy that letters fall easily by the wayside, but too many of us believe the lies we've always heard. We are convinced that we don't have anything interesting to say. This is not an easy mindset to overcome, and conquering it generally requires conversation. You may ask someone to write only to have them insist they have nothing to say. Yet, once they start talking, they may speak of the wonderful time they had on last Saturday's walk in the woods and how lovely the autumn leaves were as they drifted to the ground. One of the most difficult tasks is helping people realize that this is *something*, and a something others will enjoy reading. It did help when I offered copies of things I had written. These pieces enabled others to see just how interesting the simplest things could be when seen through someone else's eyes.

If, even after the phone calls, submissions come too slowly, you might compose a follow-up letter containing a list of topic suggestions, helpful hints, and a variety of pieces from what you've already received. Including others' submissions could further your purpose in more ways than one. First, it would give people a better idea of what you want. Second, it could encourage healthy competition ("I could do better than that!"); either result gets you more stories. Remember, also, to suggest that they go through old photos, souvenirs, letters, diaries, and anything else that might trigger hidden memories.

So — you will make phone calls, write letters, do interviews (either in person or on the phone), whatever it takes. In all of this effort, do not forget to record your own memories! Always remember that you, as well as the rest of the family, have a story to tell — no matter how young or old you are.

More Than Just Stories

The following list suggests a few things you may wish to include in your family book.

- Factual stories (of course)
- Profiles or biographies of individuals
- Written portraits - similar to biographies, but more like written 'snapshots' of a person caught in a common pose
- Letters
- Excerpts from historical documents (letters, deeds, wills, journals, receipts, etc.)
- Poetry
- A genealogy
- A family directory
- Family members' and ancestors' occupations
- Family members' and ancestors' hobbies
- Family traditions
- Funny things the children have said
- Children's explanations of why things are the way they are
- Prices, fashions, news, etc. during applicable eras
- Family members' favorites (movies, music, quotes, vacations...)
- Favorite recipes (with any attached stories... ie., my aunt cannot think of WWII without remembering Chess Pie)
- Photographs
- Family members' artwork
- Meaning of the family name
- How family members' names were chosen
- Histories of the towns/areas the family has lived in
- Maps of these areas
- Floor plans of important family homes
- Maps of your family's migration across the country or around the world
- Cards received from relatives and friends (valentines, birthday cards, etc.)
- Names and stories of friends you and family members hold dear
- Handwriting samples
- Family members' dreams (visions for their future that may not have come to pass) — Did your grandfather want to be a famous airplane pilot? Perhaps your grandmother wanted to design clothes.
- Report cards from school
- Favorite fictional stories
- Notorious tall tales

Chapter 4

So, I've Got the Stories. Now What?

We have already discussed the value of actually telling the stories. For the sake of preservation, and to touch far-flung relatives, you may consider making audio or video recordings of some of your story-telling sessions. Always remember — guard the masters; hand out the copies.

Family newsletters are not only an excellent forum for the stories, but a wonderful way to keep the family talking as well. A newsletter could be as simple as photocopies of each submission or as fancy as a multi-page publication that verges on magazine quality. Those with computers have seemingly endless options available in the realm of word processing and desktop publishing software; they could have as much fun playing with the newsletter's format as they do its content.

Family newsletters are personal things, to be adapted to your own needs and goals. What you include will be up to you and your assistants (Please let the children be involved!). I would recommend using your newsletter to gather even more stories and to acquire genealogical information as well. Genealogy is, in a sense, the tree the tales hang upon. It puts the stories in context, making them more meaningful, even as the stories bring the genealogy to life.

Those who choose the permanent option, to create a book of your family's heritage, face two choices. Do you have the book printed professionally, or do you handle things yourself? I deal primarily with the latter, but I did take time to do some research on professional printing.

Taking it to a Printer

Never having worked with a printer, I took my questions to Trudy Palmer, self-published author of *The Gift of Reading*. Our discussion and my own research made it quite clear that I could not possibly cover the vast amount of information I would need in order to have my work published professionally. There are simply too many variables, too much information to absorb before I would be prepared to deal with publishing companies.

Trudy suggests you begin by contacting self-published authors. She and her husband called every self-published author they knew of, most of whom were more than willing to share their experiences. Some of these people used techniques that did not apply to the type of book she was planning, but often they offered names of other authors and publishers who could help.

Having some experience with publishing already, her husband handled contacting the most highly recommended publishers. He began by asking pertinent questions and requesting their scales, which are used to determine the number of pages a book will contain when printed on the company's presses. These scales are of vital importance, because you must know how many pages (including blank pages) your book will contain before any publisher will quote you a price. You must also bear in mind that publishers do not print books with random numbers of pages but in signatures. A signature is generally 32 pages, which means that most books are printed in 32 page increments.

A major factor affecting price is the number of copies you require. Most printers can not make enough money on small runs, therefore 500 copies will be much more expensive per copy than will 1,000. Other factors that affect price are book size and type (paper back or hard back), paper type and weight, the cover, illustrations, and photographs. Photographs, especially, can add to the price as they require special handling.

One thing Trudy strongly recommended is that you not sign any contracts without first having the publisher send sample copies of books made like your own. Examining the sample books will help you visualize the finished product the way the publisher sees it, and this is vitally important. You must be certain that you are both "speaking the same language" or you risk taking shipment of a vast number of books that are not what you were expecting — no refunds.

Throughout my research, I came across one warning repeatedly. Book after book made a point of suggesting that you stay away from "subsidy" or "vanity" publishers, as their sole purpose seems to be relieving authors of their money. This is a complicated issue, which I will not pursue, but I felt it important to pass along the warning.

Should you desire books on the subject, check at your local library or bookstore. The one book I found to be most helpful is *The Complete Guide to Self-Publishing* by Tom and Marilyn Ross. It seems to be one of the most readily available books on self-publishing and is quite thorough. Another book I have recently learned of is *The*

Self-Publishing Manual by Dan Poynter. Its subtitle is *How to Write, Print, and Sell Your Own Book.* While I have not seen this book, it comes highly recommended by one whose judgment I trust.

This chapter, as I said earlier, cannot truly cover everything you need to know about publishing. If your desire is to see your book professionally printed then, by all means, pursue the issue. Just realize that the amount of money you will be investing and your goal of a truly professional book sets you in a different realm from the one I have traveled. I simply do not have the experience to offer the advice you need and would not presume, considering the consequences, to offer potentially incomplete advice as the final word. Get out there, ask questions, read, and enjoy yourself.

If, on the other hand, you choose to see this thing through from beginning to end as I did, read on.

Publishing At Home

Now that you know you want a book, what type of book do you want? To some extent you will have already decided this issue. Is your goal a simple book for your immediate family ("me, my four, no more")? If so, simply make a single copy of each story (handwritten or typewritten) and insert it in a common notebook or folder. This may be the best way to start. By keeping it out in the open for all to read, you may inspire others to contribute stories of their own. There are many options available if you want something fancier. Use typing or copy paper folded in half and stapled together with, perhaps, a wallpaper cover. You can have full-sized sheets of paper comb-bound into a casual book. It would be simple to photocopy pages and mail them to others who then purchase their own loose-leaf notebooks, allowing for additions... The list is limited only by your imagination and available supplies or funds.

For my family book I photocopied the pages onto 20 LB copy paper. I have since learned that the ideal, when printing on both sides, is to use 50 LB paper. Anything lighter tends to allow the copy on one side of the paper to show through to the reverse side. While 50 LB may be a bit much in my case, I will certainly consider something heavier than 20 for the next book we publish.

I chose an 80 LB card stock for the cover. I used 80 LB because I liked this particular paper, but lighter paper (67 LB for instance) may have worked as well. I do want the cover to be considerably sturdier than the body, however, so I will probably use 80 LB or heavier with the next book. Yes, this may mean having the cover printed by one of my local printers, but it might be worth the investment. We shall see.

The next step was to stack the pages and cover, fold them all in half and staple the lot together. This made a 5 ½" by 8 ½" book that was relatively inexpensive and looks fairly professional. I chose this format because I wanted more stories than I was getting and felt that getting copies out might whet everyone's appetites. My address is in the forward along with an invitation to all, both young and old, to send in their stories. My hope was that relatives would read the stories, decide they could write at least as well as those who had already submitted, and send in stories of their own.

My ultimate goal was to eventually put together a 'real' book and have it printed professionally, yet I soon began to wonder if this would be the best thing for us. Even after I stopped taking submissions for the first book, one aunt and I were still writing. Now we are doing something I touched on earlier. It is a simple thing to include, with the family newsletter, 5½" by 8½" pages containing the latest submissions. This way, everyone purchases the small loose-leaf notebooks that are available at office supply stores and inserts the new stories as they arrive. Use a heavier paper if you do this, so the pages will take more abuse, and mail them in envelopes large enough that you need not fold the story pages. This is not the professional look I had desired. It also lacks a table of contents and index. It is readily expandable, however, and not nearly as expensive as printing a book. If you charge a small subscription fee to cover copying and postage, it becomes more manageable still. These pages are also the same size as our family book, allowing everyone to punch holes in the book and insert it in the same notebook, thereby keeping all stories together.

Dealing With Details

Now let's discuss the 'nuts and bolts' of what I did. I have a computer and I have found in recent years that computers handle a seemingly endless variety of tasks. I will not even begin to get into all they are capable of or how to make them do it, especially since you may well know more than I do. If, by chance, you are a computer novice, you face one of the best learning experiences there is. Trust me, I knew almost nothing about wordprocessing and absolutely nothing about desktop publishing when I began my family book. I went through some intense "on the job training" and came out of it quite pleased with what I had learned. I am not recommending that those who have no computer run out and invest in one for this project. You can still do what I've done, but it will simply take a little more time and effort on your part.

Having the computer, I was free to wait before making any definite decisions about book format. I simply set up a file and entered the stories as they came in, without worrying about page sizes or anything else. This allowed me to wait until I knew how many stories I was dealing with before I settled on the book's layout. If you will be using a typewriter, you need to make these decisions first and type submissions in the proper format as you work your way through them. I will also point out that you do have another option — to photocopy things exactly as you receive them. Depending on the book format you use, this may require a copier that enlarges and reduces, but most commercial copiers handle these tasks easily. Doing this would preserve the stories in their original form and may be a wonderful option. (If I had actually photocopied my grandmother's letter, for instance — how special that would have been)! It is probable, however, that even if you choose this option some letters will be too difficult to decipher. These you will need to type up if you expect anyone to read them.

Having decided to make a simple folded book, I knew that my pages would be 5 ½" by 8 ½." To clarify, I stacked 12 sheets of paper and folded them in half, making each page be 5 ½" by 8 ½" (half of an 8 ½" by 11" sheet of paper). This meant that each sheet of paper had two book pages on each side and the twelve folded sheets of paper gave me a 48 page book. I then, of course, put the cover on the outside.

Knowing my page size, I set my margins and began formatting what I had typed in. Once I had given the computer the details concerning page size, margins, tabs, etc., I started playing around with the stories. The first step was to determine their order. I wanted them separated into general categories (although I did not label them as categories) so the reader would not feel he was jumping from one topic to another. In general, my book fell into childhood stories (which I placed in order of generation — my grandmother's, my mother's, my own), engagement/marriage stories, "portraits", and stories that defied these categories. Having separated them into rough categories and placed those categories in order, I then put each category's submissions in order. I did my best to mix things up so there would not be any one long string of stories by the same author. Also, I was flexible. Although I separated the childhood stories by generation, I felt a poem I had written would be a great introduction to this section so I put it in the very front of the group.

Now that my stories were in order I started "dressing them up." With the computer I had such an incredible selection of fonts (type styles) and sizes that I hardly knew where to begin. I considered the feel I wanted for several days before I did anything. I knew I wanted something old-fashioned that would make people think of a book that had been around for years and years, holding intriguing secrets. Having always appreciated the Victorian tendency to combine a tremendous number of type styles on the same page, I opted to use the trick myself and began with the title page. I considered many possible titles before finally settling on my favorite, *YESTERDAY*. I put the title on one line and the subtitle, *A Family Treasury*, on the next. Then I dropped down several lines and typed "collected by" on another line and "Tammy Marshall Cardwell" on the last. I was familiar enough with the available fonts to know I preferred one over all the others. I put the title in this font and made it as large as I felt I dared. Then I started playing around with the other three lines, working toward the best possible combination of type styles and sizes. (See Figure 1)

Figure 1: *Title Page*

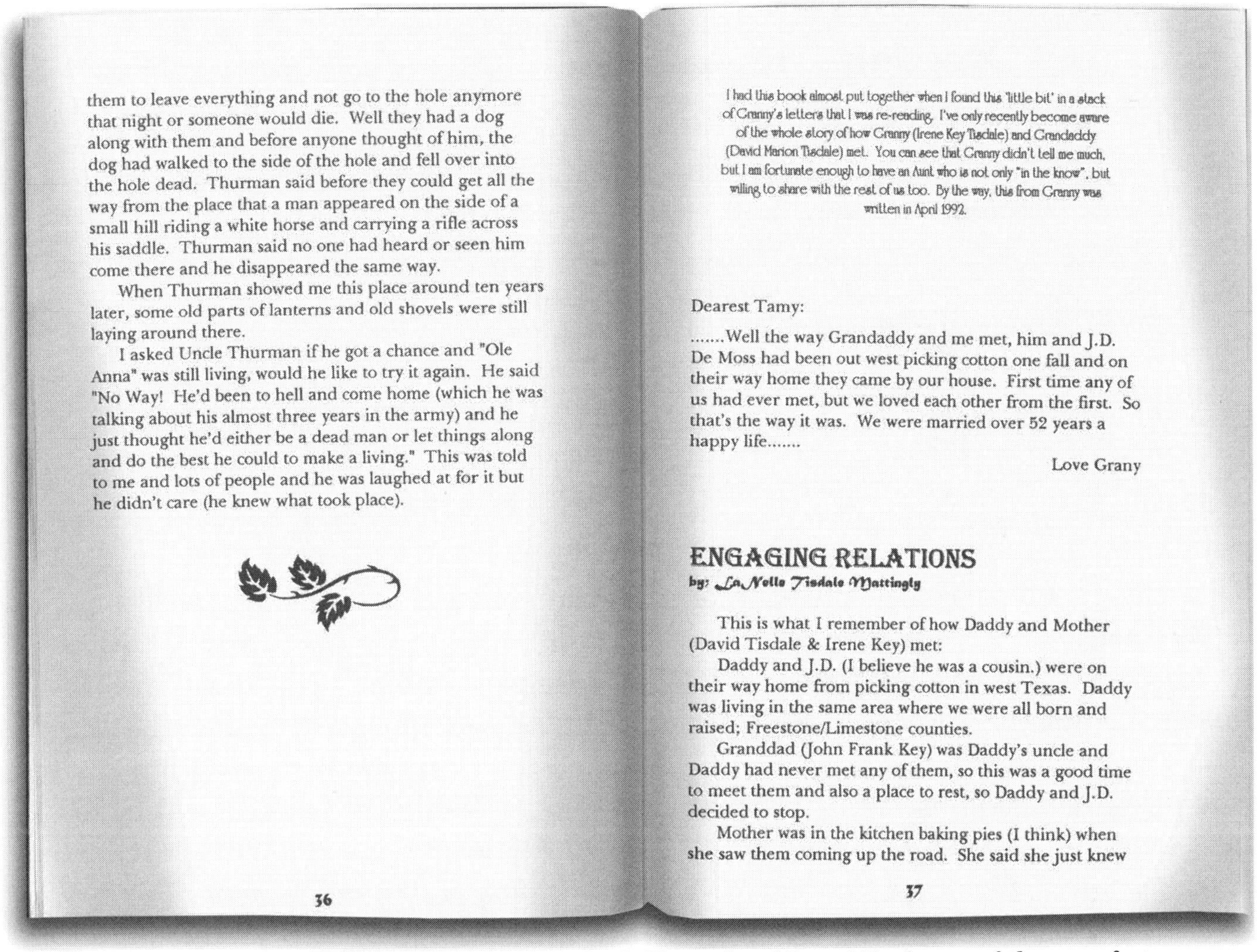

them to leave everything and not go to the hole anymore that night or someone would die. Well they had a dog along with them and before anyone thought of him, the dog had walked to the side of the hole and fell over into the hole dead. Thurman said before they could get all the way from the place that a man appeared on the side of a small hill riding a white horse and carrying a rifle across his saddle. Thurman said no one had heard or seen him come there and he disappeared the same way.

When Thurman showed me this place around ten years later, some old parts of lanterns and old shovels were still laying around there.

I asked Uncle Thurman if he got a chance and "Ole Anna" was still living, would he like to try it again. He said "No Way! He'd been to hell and come home (which he was talking about his almost three years in the army) and he just thought he'd either be a dead man or let things along and do the best he could to make a living." This was told to me and lots of people and he was laughed at for it but he didn't care (he knew what took place).

36

I had this book almost put together when I found this 'little bit' in a stack of Granny's letters that I was re-reading. I've only recently become aware of the whole story of how Granny (Irene Key Tisdale) and Grandaddy (David Marion Tisdale) met. You can see that Granny didn't tell me much, but I am fortunate enough to have an Aunt who is not only "in the know", but willing to share with the rest of us too. By the way, this from Granny was written in April 1992.

Dearest Tamy:

.......Well the way Grandaddy and me met, him and J.D. De Moss had been out west picking cotton one fall and on their way home they came by our house. First time any of us had ever met, but we loved each other from the first. So that's the way it was. We were married over 52 years a happy life.......

Love Grany

ENGAGING RELATIONS

by: LaNelle Tisdale Mattingly

This is what I remember of how Daddy and Mother (David Tisdale & Irene Key) met:

Daddy and J.D. (I believe he was a cousin.) were on their way home from picking cotton in west Texas. Daddy was living in the same area where we were all born and raised; Freestone/Limestone counties.

Granddad (John Frank Key) was Daddy's uncle and Daddy had never met any of them, so this was a good time to meet them and also a place to rest, so Daddy and J.D. decided to stop.

Mother was in the kitchen baking pies (I think) when she saw them coming up the road. She said she just knew

37

Figure 2: *This is a page excerpt from the author's book,* Yesterday *(Page 37). the top of the page features a letter written to the author (excerpted below) and the bottom of the page illustrates her use of various font styles and sizes (excerpted on the next page).*

Excerpt from Figure 2 (top of page):

I had this book almost put together when I found this 'little bit' in a stack of Granny's letters that I was re-reading. I've only recently become aware of the whole story of how Granny (Irene Key Tisdale) and Grandaddy (David Marion Tisdale) met. You can see that Granny didn't tell me much, but I am fortunate enough to have an Aunt who is not only "in the know", but willing to share with the rest of us too. By the way, this from Granny was written in April 1992.

Dearest Tamy:

Well the way Grandaddy and me met, him and J.D. DeMoss had been out west picking cotton one fall and on their way home they came by our house. First time any of us had ever met, but we loved each other from the first. So that's the way it was. We were married over 52 years a happy life...

Love Grany

Excerpt from Figure 2:

Use of type fonts in Figure 2:

Engaging Relations

(Large display or "fancy" Font)

by LaNelle Tisdale Mattingly

(smaller display font italic)

This is what I remember of how Daddy and Mother (David Tisdale & Irene Key) met:

(Body Copy font)

Daddy and J.D. (I believe he was a cousin.) were on their way home from picking cotton in west Texas. Daddy was living in the same area where we were all born and raised; Freestone/Limestone counties.

Granddad (John Frank Key) was Daddy's uncle and Daddy had never met any of them, so this was a good time to meet them and also a place to rest, so Daddy and J.D. decided to stop.

Achieving balance in a project like this is not an easy thing and requires an investment of time, but I consider what I put into it to be time well spent. Once I determined what combination to use on the title page, it took little effort to decide about the body of the book. I put story titles in the same font as I had the book title. I also used the same font on the authors' bylines as I had used on my own name on the title page. I worked for balance when it came to sizing the fonts in both titles and bylines. I was especially careful to make the titles large enough to set them out as titles, but not so large that they became obnoxious. I did not get fancy on the stories themselves. I used a basic font that is clear enough to read easily in large blocks. (See figure 2). One option I did have, but did not take advantage of, is the use of dropped caps. This is where the first letter of a paragraph or chapter is larger than the text, taking up three lines or so. It gives added interest and is common in books we would now consider antiques.

At this point I faced the graphics decision. My husband really likes clip art and had several files of assorted pictures, frames, etc. just waiting to be inserted wherever I wanted them. I did try several things but found that I preferred a simpler approach. I chose one graphic image and used it consistently throughout the book to separate the different story types. I did not label the separations; I used the graphic because I wanted to be subtle. After studying the completed book, I've decided this manner of marking the separation is too subtle to work well. If I had it to do over again, I would use it after every story.

There are those who might say I don't know when to "leave well enough alone," and they may be right. As I read some things, I found I just had to comment on them. I felt some letters needed explanation and that the reader should know when stories were written during significant time periods. Whatever the reason, I simply could not keep my mouth shut (or pen still — as the case may be). I took the advantage all editors have and added Editor's Notes. I put these notes either before or after the story, wherever I felt they would add interest, and I put them in a totally different, smaller font. I wanted them to be heard, but I did not want them to yell and scream. (See Figure 2).

I will tell on myself here and admit that I overlooked one small detail when I put my family book together. I forgot to include the date of publication. One would think such a fundamental thing as this would almost include itself, but I blew it and left myself the onerous task of writing in each book the words "Printed February 1994." I suggest you remember to put these words (or similar ones) into the manuscript before you print it.

Now the book had very much fallen together, needing only a little fine tuning. I adjusted page breaks to avoid having stories carry over to the next page by only one or two lines. I even lengthened some of my own stories at the last minute, to help fill things out. In the end, I was glad I had; these stories improved greatly as a result. Finally, I went through the manuscript several times to make sure my editor's notes, titles, bylines, and graphics were consistent in size and spacing. I also had a willing aunt read and proof copy after copy. Do have at least one other person help proof your manuscript. No matter how good you are, you are likely to miss things. To be honest, I have found several typographical errors in the finished book.

The next step may not be absolutely necessary for those who have computers and know how to use them, but I was a novice at best and chose to allow no room for error. I ran a copy of everything I had, including the title page, the dedication (definitely include a dedication), and the header for the "Final Notes" section in which I intended to place a genealogy.

I calculated the number of pages I needed for my book, allowing for blank pages at the beginning and end as well as the not yet written Table of Contents. I needed 48 pages and intended to use both the front and back of every page, so I pulled out 12 sheets of paper for the body and one extra for the cover then stapled them together. I wrote the word "Yesterday" on the cover so I would know which end was up and proceeded to cut up all of my pages and glue them into this dummy book. This gave me an absolutely dead-on, can't-go-wrong way to number my pages and supplied a pattern that I would later use to make my photocopy masters.

With my page numbers finalized, I went back and created a table of contents (utilizing the same selection of fonts found throughout the book). The computer would have generated the Table of Contents for me, but I had no idea how to talk it

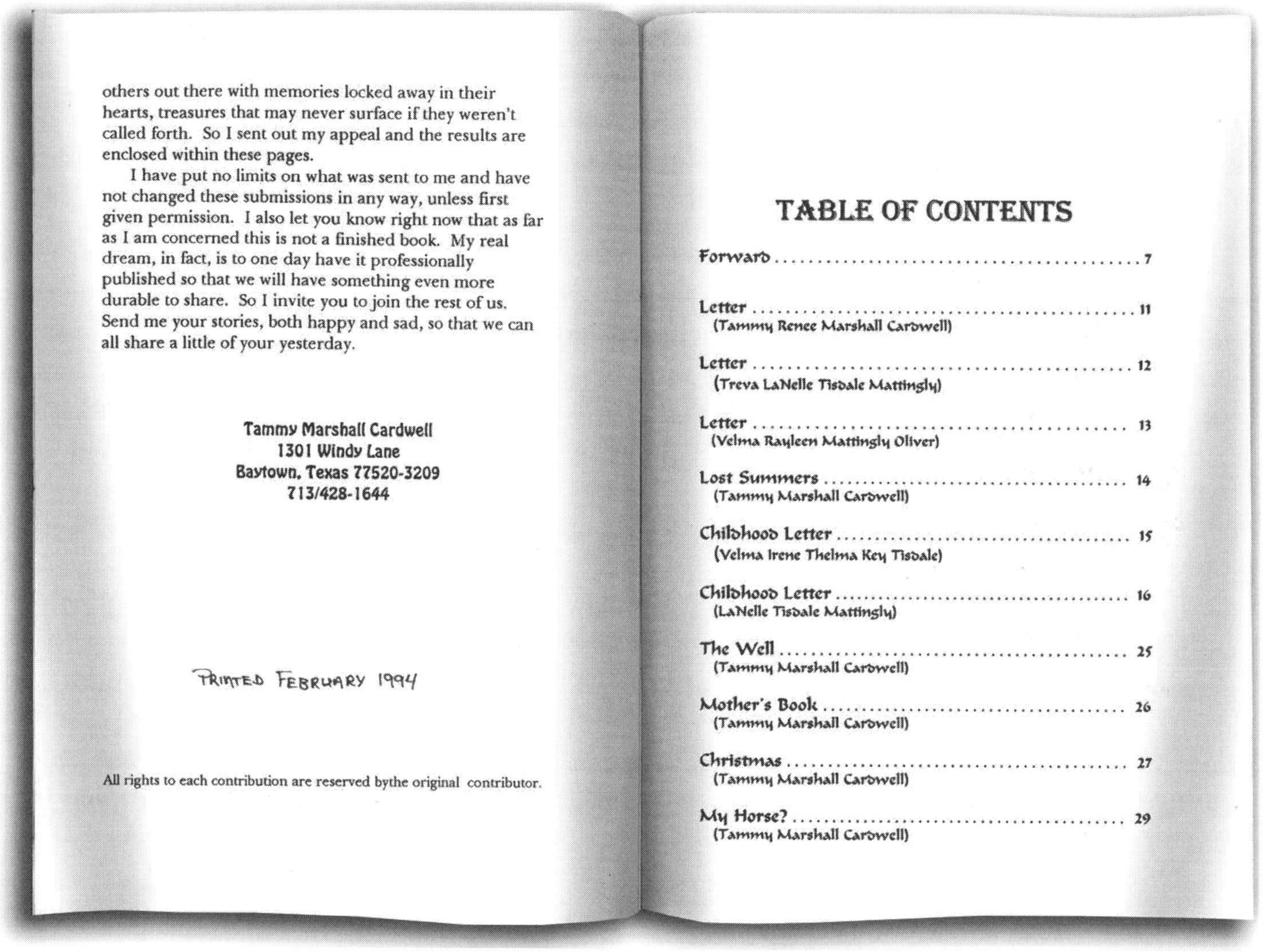

others out there with memories locked away in their hearts, treasures that may never surface if they weren't called forth. So I sent out my appeal and the results are enclosed within these pages.

I have put no limits on what was sent to me and have not changed these submissions in any way, unless first given permission. I also let you know right now that as far as I am concerned this is not a finished book. My real dream, in fact, is to one day have it professionally published so that we will have something even more durable to share. So I invite you to join the rest of us. Send me your stories, both happy and sad, so that we can all share a little of your yesterday.

Tammy Marshall Cardwell
1301 Windy Lane
Baytown, Texas 77520-3209
713/428-1644

PRINTED FEBRUARY 1994

All rights to each contribution are reserved bythe original contributor.

TABLE OF CONTENTS

Figure 3: *Table of Contents*

into doing the job. Not having access to my husband's expertise at the time, and not wanting to wait, I did it by hand. My table of contents is similar to those found in any book. The one thing I did do "my way" concerns the authors' names. I felt it important to include everyone's full name (including unused middle and maiden names) to assist those who might be unsure of relationships. I also felt it would complement the genealogy I had planned to include in the "Final Notes" section. Using a person's full name throughout the book proved to be impractical. (Granny's name was Velma Irene Thelma Key Tisdale — for instance) I chose instead to include the full name in the table of contents the first time it appeared, and to use common names thereafter (making it clear that both were the same person, naturally). (See Figure 3).I set no rules here, simply offer advice. The more complete name avoids any confusion as to the author's identity. Some names, however, are so cumbersome and/or different from the name actually used that I feel it is appropriate to include both where possible. The genealogy, by the way, did not make it into the book. I'd not done sufficient research to warrant including a genealogy so I chose, instead, to put out a plea for information in hopes that I might include a respectable genealogy in the next edition.

Cover design was the next step in the actual computer work. Jack knew just what I wanted, so I was able to leave it completely in his hands. The style was simple. He copied the title page I had previously created and put a frame around it. The frame, while being ornate, does not detract from the title in any way and makes for a beautiful cover. (See Figure 4). You have many options available when you are ready to design your cover. You can design your own cover or have a family member do it. If you choose, you might even hire a graphic artist. Many schools have graphic arts students who need projects and would be willing to work on your cover for, perhaps, a very small fee.

Jack did do one last bit of manipulation in the computer. I obviously needed to have the pages be sideways on the paper (two pages per sheet). This involved changing the printer setting from "portrait" to "landscape". This gave me a stack of papers, each containing one book page printed on the right side of the paper. After he printed them all on an ink jet printer, I pulled out the dummy book I had created earlier and used it as a pattern to build the masters.

Putting it Together

The following steps, though not so difficult in practice, are a challenge to explain on paper. While you may be a little confused the first time you read them, you should "catch on" when you actually have your own papers in front of you and can work with them.

I stood at a table on which I placed my dummy book, the pages Jack had given me, a pair of scissors and a roll of tape. I removed the staples from the dummy book and laid it open flat with the cover on top. I then removed the cover and the flyleaf (the blank sheet of paper just inside the cover) so that I could see the first printed page, and I began building my masters.

To do this I would look at the sheet that was face up on the dummy book, find the appropriate pages (the printed copies of the two pages that were showing) and tape them together. This involved cutting the excess paper off one of the sheets and taping that page onto the excess paper of the other sheet. When I had finished, and my master matched the sheet in the dummy book, I would lay the master face down on the table. Then I flipped the dummy sheet over (face down) so that I could see

Figure 4: *The Cover of* Yesterday, A Family Treasury

which pages were showing on its back side. I would then build the master for the back side in the same manner as I had the master for the front. When this master was complete, I would lay it face up on top of the one I had assembled earlier. If I were to pick up these two masters just as I had laid them down (back to back), they would match the front and back of the dummy sheet. I used tape because it was all I had, but glue stick works much better. You may also choose to glue the two master-sheets together so the front and back will not be accidentally separated.

Having finished with that particular dummy sheet, I would then lay it on the discarded dummy pile (where I had put the cover and flyleaf earlier) and work on masters to match the front and back of the next dummy sheet. In this manner I worked my way through the entire book until I had a stack of masters matching the sheets in the dummy stack. I then presented Jack with these masters and sent him off to do his "copier magic."

He took these masters with him to work the next day. Since the machine at his office could copy both sides of the paper at the same time, he first copied a set of masters in which both front and back were on the same sheet of paper. This is not absolutely necessary, but it does help with this type of copier because you work with one sheet of paper instead of multiple sheets glued together.

Copying the body of the book took several hours, but was not difficult. The cover, on the other hand, was a major frustration. I had selected a paper that, for whatever reason, would not work in this machine and I had to find a copier that could handle it. I eventually found a company that had the right machine and charged less than 2 cents per copy, which excited me because the usual rate around here is 5 cents, even when I supply my own paper.

While waiting for the copies, I also bought a stapler. I had learned with my dummy book that a standard stapler would not reach the middle of the paper. We had hoped to find a larger stapler and borrow it, but we'd had no success. When I found a Stanley® Bostitch 12" long-reach stapler for under $25.00, I decided it was worth investing in. I would have had to hire a printer to staple the books for me otherwise and felt that this savings, with anything I may need it for later, made it an excusable expense. It is one purchase I have never regretted. I've come to the conclusion that almost every house needs one of these gems.

Jack advised prefolding the covers and pages before I stapled them. He suggested that this would avoid the problems I'd had with the dummy book. (The darned thing wouldn't stay closed). I took his advice, of course, and prefolding the sheets did make all the difference.

At this point my book was complete, or as complete as I could get it. I do wish I had taken the time to compile and include at least a good start on a genealogy. I also wish I had remembered to include a family directory. I had fully intended to do so, but forgot all about it until we were too far into the publishing process. Another regret I have is that I lacked the money to invest in pictures. Today's color copiers do such a tremendous job with photographs that I could have inserted some in the middle of the book if I had not been on such a shoestring budget. The budget problem may be my own fault. It is possible that my family would have pitched in to help financially. Unfortunately, I was prideful enough that I never asked, and the donation one aunt made was, while certainly helpful, not enough to make the difference.

You may have your own regrets when you've finished your book. There may be elements you must leave out or you may lack the proper equipment to do things as you wish. I do not believe, however, that you will regret the book itself or the time you've invested in it. There have been few projects, very few, that have left me as satisfied as this one. As much as I wish I had included the items I've mentioned leaving out, only one thing really upsets me. I made one mistake I am determined not to make again; I left my children out of the process. This book was intended for them, to bring our family closer together than ever before. Why didn't it occur to me that they, too, should have a part? Make this truly a family affair. Bring in even the youngest children and let them illustrate the stories the older children and adults write. Involve as many relatives as possible, both the young and the old, in all aspects of the project. I don't think you will regret this either.

Chapter 5

But Wait! What About a Genealogy?

You have seen how much I regret leaving the genealogy out of my family book. I have recently begun work on my genealogy, and it is every bit as exciting as collecting the stories. Learning certain things about my ancestors' relationships gives the stories more depth as well, making them much more vital and important to me. I am only a novice myself, but I want you to see how easy it is to begin and how many resources there are to help you on your way. In this chapter I will share some things I have learned, as well as a few resources, in hopes that it will encourage you to search out your own roots.

The first step in researching your genealogy is to talk to your relatives and go through all of the family Bibles, letters, scrapbooks, diaries, legal documents, etc. that you can get your hands on. The most important things you are looking for are names, dates (death, marriage, birth and other significant dates), and places of residence. You will also want to save other information about these people, as well as photos whenever possible. The rule is 'don't throw anything away.' Not only is there always the possibility that a previously unacknowledged scrap of information may prove invaluable in the search, but these scraps also give you insights into the personalities and lives of your ancestors. You can see how genealogy and family tales go hand in hand. The tales bring the names and dates to life and the names and dates clarify the tales, especially by explaining the relationships between your stories' subjects. It astonished me, for example, to learn that my grandparents were not distantly related, but were actually second cousins. When I was melding information from his family with information from her family, I found that they shared the same great-grandfather.

I began my search in much the same way as I had begun my story search. With every copy of the family book I sent out, I also sent a plea for more information. I also sent one copy to a distant relative. I had learned that she handled the Key family reunion (Key is a big name in my family) and felt she would be the most likely candidate for "keeper of the genealogy." I was proven right when I received a detailed copy of what she had regarding my grandfather's maternal family.

The next step was to call people after they'd had time to read the book. The stories have a wonderful tendency to bring to mind forgotten details, and a few carefully asked questions bring other hidden facts to light. There are plenty of the usual questions. "Do you remember where and when he was born?" "Who did he marry?" "When did he move to Texas?" These are important, but you will also want to ask less obvious questions like... "Why did they move to Texas?" "How did his parents react when he took their only grandchildren away?" "What was life like in their new home?" "Did life there live up to their expectations?"

Obviously, what was for me a second step can be a first step for you. Ask relatives for genealogical information at the same time you ask for stories, knowing that the search for one type of information might well lead to the other. Ask relatives to compile a pedigree (See Figure 5) going back as far as they can. Also ask them for the current addresses of as many relatives as possible. You will want these addresses anyway; it is just one more area in which genealogy and family tales overlap.

Finding Your Ancestors

One thing you must remember, as you gather information, is that the cemetery is the only place you will find things written in stone, and even tombstones have been known to be wrong. Get confirmation. Seek out two or three "witnesses." I received a surprisingly extensive pedigree, but I will accept no names or dates as givens until I get my hands on primary sources. By primary sources I mean family Bibles, obituaries, death records, birth records, military records, wills, deeds, etc. One tool you may wish to get your hands on is The *Handy Book for Genealogists* by Everton Publishers (See Appendix B). This is probably one of the tools most used by genealogists. In it you will find a state-by-state, county-by-county guide to obtaining vital records. It even tells you what records are available in which offices, making note of records that have been destroyed or lost. My only problem is that my library classifies this book as a reference tool, meaning I can't check it out. I will likely find myself purchasing it before long.

Everton's Genealogical Helper, also by Everton Publishers, is a magazine specifically designed to assist those involved in searches. Here you will find countless ads placed by individuals looking for information, either specific or general, about their ancestors. You will also find ads for companies that have family group sheets in stock (See Figure 6), and you may find your family among their records. The magazine also contains ads for companies who want to publish your family story. I have not called about any of these ads to find out how they do business, but it may be well worth investigating if you do not wish to do all of the work yourself. However, as I warned earlier, you would be wise to steer away from any companies that are, in fact, subsidy or "vanity" presses. This type of press seems to exist only to relieve the author of as much money as possible. Sadly, the author may end up not even owning the very books for which he has paid such a high price.

Your library might also have books listing family associations, how-to books on genealogy, genealogy magazines, old maps, directories of genealogical and historical societies, phone books, old newspapers, ships' passenger lists, and much more. You may even be fortunate enough to encounter a helpful librarian or fellow researcher who will start you on your way.

One thing you will look for in your search is obituaries. These generally include birth date and place, marriage date and place, parent's names, surviving siblings and descendants, cemetery information and biographical material. You will also seek out such things as death, marriage, divorce and birth records (Genealogists suggest starting with death and working backwards.), probate and land records, wills, newspaper articles, county history biographies, census records, military records, school records, etc..

You can do much of your research by letter. Many of the places you will deal with would rather mail you the information, and postage generally runs much less than travel expenses. County records are vital. These will typically have birth, death, marriage, divorce, probate, and land records. Historical and genealogical societies and libraries might have obituaries (you will need a death date), cemetery records (tremendous resources), newspaper articles (larger libraries may have articles indexed by surname), marriage records, church records, information from published county and city histories, wills, names of other people who are researching along the same lines, and published family histories. Church records can be extensive or not; it depends on the church. You do stand a good chance of finding information on baptisms, marriages, burials, and membership, and (perhaps best of all) letters of transference. Letters of transference tell you where this particular ancestor came from, which is a piece of much needed information. You may also find birth, marriage, and death records at the state Bureau of Vital Statistics.

One of the most exciting places to go in your ancestor search is The Family History Library in Salt Lake City, Utah [See Appendix B]. The Church of Jesus

Christ of Latter-day Saints has an almost unbelievable wealth of information stored in this complex, and they make it readily available. In an effort to make their information accessible to as many as possible, the Family History Library has opened Family History Centers across the country. You can find these centers by contacting the library or by looking in your phone book for the words "Church of Jesus Christ of Latter-day Saints — Family History Center." We have several in the Houston area, so Jack and I visited one of those closest to us.

We knew little about what the center had to offer, but we had heard about Ancestral File™ and knew we wanted to use it, so we made an appointment for an hour on their computer. Many who access listings in Ancestral File™ are astonished to find large family group sheets that other researchers have already compiled. It is possible that you might be able to go in and download such a pedigree (family tree) and be relieved of years of work. The only thing you must be aware of is that people compiled these pedigrees, and people sometimes make mistakes. No matter what information you receive, do not consider it absolute until you have it backed up with records.

The centers offer much more, including other computer options. The computers usually have time limits, because of the demand. Even if you cannot access a computer, there are other sources of research available. You even have the option of paying a small fee to 'borrow' records from the library in Salt Lake City.

You could easily lose yourself in one of these centers for days at a time. Be prepared to spend most of your first trip familiarizing yourself with the center and the tools available. We came away disappointed that we found so little in the two hours we were there, but it took some time to become comfortable with everything. By the way, we were not among those fortunate ones who find complete pedigrees. Apparently names like Tisdale, Cardwell, Key, Marshall and Perry don't grow on trees — not the right ones anyway.

There are many more tools and sources of help available, including the National Genealogical Society. For more listings, as well as names and addresses, see appendix B.

Computer Helps

Genealogy software abounds, but you will want to select your program carefully. One of the most important factors to look for is GEDCOM, which is the universal genealogy data base. GEDCOM enables you to import and export information from compatible software, saving untold hours of entering records by hand.

Jack and I have used an older version of Family Tree Maker™ for Windows™, put out by Broderbund Software (Banner Blue division). We paid about $40.00, and have been quite pleased with it. It allows us to store and retrieve large amounts of information at will, works with our word processing program, supports GEDCOM, and creates beautiful charts. We were fortunate in our selection, since we had no idea what we were looking at when we purchased it. There are several excellent programs out there. Reviews of some products are in appendix B.

Computers with modems can access any of a number of genealogy Bulletin Board Services (BBS's). Genealogy BBSs are listed in numerous magazines and often in local papers. The major on-line companies offer genealogy forums as well. The services available vary; most have libraries from which you can download almost anything from genealogical software and form generators to lists of resource addresses and available genealogies. They almost always offer message areas where you can link up with others to exchange information. You have many fellow researchers who will gladly share from their records. The understanding is that you will be equally as helpful when you have something someone else needs. Prices for accessing BBS's and on-line services vary from 'free' to several dollars an hour. Check around and see what works for you.

The Paperwork

If you do not use a computer, perhaps even if you do, you should purchase or design certain forms that will make your record keeping easier. You will need a Pedigree Chart, the traditional "family tree" that begins with you and works backwards. (See Figure 5). Each entry is numbered. For example: You are #1, your father is #2, your mother is #3, your father's father is #4, your father's mother is #5, etc. This will contain the "bare bones" information and give you a quick overview of relationships. You will also need to keep Family Group Sheets (See Figure 6), which track pertinent information on the husband, the wife, and the children. A new spouse calls for a new Family Group Sheet.

You will find it most helpful to keep a file on each of these people. You might wish to track them by number, as well as by name, so that you can more easily relate all information back to the Pedigree Chart. This also protects you from the risk of being confused by two different ancestors who have the same name. You will want to include a Biographical Worksheet (See Figure 7) in each file. This worksheet contains all of the statistical information you have on this ancestor. You should also keep a list of the sources you used in your search, including notes identifying the holders of family bibles and other important artifacts. This file is also where you will store any other information you acquire such as certificates, wills, photographs, letters, etc. Be careful with these historical items; proper care and preservation is a must. Use archive safe envelopes and sleeves whenever possible. Archive safe products protect important documents from acid migration, which is deadly to paper.

When ready to publish the genealogy, you will begin as far back as you can and come forward, listing your earliest ancestor's descendants. Your local library may well have copies of others' genealogies and you would be wise to examine them. Determine the format that works best for you and decide how much information to include in the genealogy itself. Some of your findings will undoubtedly develop into stories that will find their way into the body of your book.

A final word. Genealogical research can be like a fever... all consuming. Enjoy it.

Your Own Stories

You can begin your genealogical adventure right away, in the comfort of your own home, by recording what you already know (your immediate family's vital statistics). To help you begin, we have included some reproducible forms for photocopying and some samples from the author's personal research. While this is only a beginning, it will let you experience how exciting even these first steps can be.

YOU
Name: ____
Place: ____
Born: ____
Place: ____
1 Married: ____
Place: ____
Died: ____
Place: ____

SPOUSE (of No.1)
Name ____

FATHER (OF NO.1)
Name: ____
Born: ____
2 Place: ____
Married: ____
Place: ____
Died: ____

MOTHER (OF NO.1)
Name: ____
Born: ____
3 Place: ____
Died: ____
Place: ____

FATHER (OF NO.2)
Name: ____
Born: ____
Place: ____
4 Married: ____
Place: ____
Died: ____
Place: ____

MOTHER (OF NO.2)
Name: ____
Born: ____
5 Place: ____
Died: ____
Place: ____

FATHER (OF NO.3)
Name: ____
Born: ____
Place: ____
6 Married: ____
Place: ____
Died: ____
Place: ____

MOTHER (OF NO.3)
Name: ____
Born: ____
7 Place: ____
Died: ____
Place: ____

(FATHER OF NO.4)
Name: ____
Born: ____
8 Place: ____
Married: ____
Place: ____
Died: ____

MOTHER (OF NO.4)
Name: ____
9 Born: ____
Place: ____
Died: ____

FATHER (OF NO.5)
Name: ____
Born: ____
10 Place: ____
Married: ____
Place: ____
Died: ____

MOTHER (OF NO.5)
Name: ____
11 Born: ____
Place: ____
Died: ____

FATHER (OF NO.6)
Name: ____
Born: ____
12 Place: ____
Married: ____
Place: ____
Died: ____

MOTHER (OF NO.6)
Name: ____
13 Born: ____
Place: ____
Died: ____

FATHER (OF NO.7)
Name: ____
Born: ____
14 Place: ____
Married: ____
Place: ____
Died: ____

Mother (of no.7)
Name: ____
15 Born: ____
Place: ____
Died: ____

Figure 5: Family Tree (or Pedigree).

Family Group Sheet

16 June 1994

HUSBAND: David Marion Tisdale

BORN: 14 August 1902 in Rabbit Hill - close to Wortham, Texas
MARRIED: 05 April 1925 in Weatherford, Texas
DIED: 25 June 1977 buried at Newhope Cemetery, Freestone County, Texas
BURIED: Newhope Cemetery, Freestone County, Texas
FATHER: William Alfred Tisdale
MOTHER: Martha Eleanor Key

WIFE: Velma Irene Thelma Key

BORN: 04 August 1907 in Dicey, Parker County, Texas
DIED: 22 August 1993 in Baytown, Harris County, Texas; buried Newhope Cemetery
BURIED: Newhope Cemetery, Freestone County, Texas
FATHER: John Franklin Key
MOTHER: Edna May Stout

CHILDREN

1. NAME: Jewell Florene Tisdale F

BORN:17 April 1926
MARR:23 March 1946 in Teague, Texas
SPOUSE:Thurman Thomas Padgett
DIED:
BURIED:

2. NAME: John Irvin Alfred Tisdale M

BORN:28 August 1929
MARR:1 June 1957
SPOUSE:Bonnie (Price) Black
DIED:
BURIED:

3. NAME: Harley Douglas Tisdale M

BORN:30 September 1932
MARR:
SPOUSE:Wanda (Osborne)
DIED:
BURIED:

4. NAME: David Lloyd Tisdale M

BORN:25(?) March 1936
MARR:
SPOUSE:
DIED:09 March 1940
BURIED:Newhope Cemetery, Freestone County, Texas

5. NAME: Treva LaNelle Tisdale F

BORN:14 October 1938 in Mexia, Freestone County, Texas
MARR:26 October 1953
SPOUSE:Marshall Ray Mattingly
DIED:
BURIED:

6. NAME: JoAnn Tisdale F

BORN:20 February 1941 at "Manning Place", Freestone County, Texas
MARR:11 September 1959 at 2nd Baptist Church, Highlands, Harris County, Texas
SPOUSE:Richard Donnell Marshall
DIED:
BURIED:

Figure 6a: Sample Family Group Sheet

Family Group Sheet

Date: ______________________________

HUSBAND: ____

BORN: ____

MARRIED: ____

DIED: ____

BURIED: ____

FATHER: ____

MOTHER: ____

WIFE: ____

BORN: ____

DIED: ____

BURIED: ____

FATHER: ____

MOTHER: ____

CHILDREN

1. NAME: ____ (M/F) ________

BORN: ____

MARRIED: ____

DIED: ____

BURIED: ____

2. NAME: ____ (M/F) ________

BORN: ____

MARRIED: ____

DIED: ____

BURIED: ____

3. NAME: ____ (M/F) ________

BORN: ____

MARRIED: ____

DIED: ____

BURIED: ____

Figure 6: Family Group Worksheet

4. NAME: ______________________________ (M/F)

BORN: ______________________________

MARRIED: ______________________________

DIED: ______________________________

BURIED: ______________________________

5. NAME: ______________________________ (M/F)

BORN: ______________________________

MARRIED: ______________________________

DIED: ______________________________

BURIED: ______________________________

6. NAME: ______________________________ (M/F)

BORN: ______________________________

MARRIED: ______________________________

DIED: ______________________________

BURIED: ______________________________

7. NAME: ______________________________ (M/F)

BORN: ______________________________

MARRIED: ______________________________

DIED: ______________________________

BURIED: ______________________________

8. NAME: ______________________________ (M/F)

BORN: ______________________________

MARRIED: ______________________________

DIED: ______________________________

BURIED: ______________________________

9. NAME: ______________________________ (M/F)

BORN: ______________________________

MARRIED: ______________________________

DIED: ______________________________

BURIED: ______________________________

Figure 6: Family Group Worksheet

Sample Biographical Worksheet

DAVID MARION TISDALE

1902: Born on 14 August in Rabbit Hill, Texas (close to Wortham) to William Alfred Tisdale and Martha Eleanor Key
1925: Married Velma Irene Thelma Key on 5 April in Weatherford, Texas
1926: Birth of Jewell Florene Tisdale on 17 April in Texas
1929: Birth of John Irvin Alfred Tisdale (Alfred is not on birth cert.) on 28 August in Texas
1932: Birth of Harley Douglas Tisdale on 30 September in Texas
1936: Birth of David Lloyd Tisdale (on 25 March?) in Texas
1938: Birth of Treva LaNelle Tisdale on 14 October in Mexia (Limestone County), Texas
1939: (circa)Served on school board at Shanks School; instrumental in establishing 1st library
1940: Death of David Lloyd 9 March in (Freestone County), Texas
1941: Birth of JoAnn Tisdale on 20 February [at the "Manning Place"] in (Freestone Co.), Texas
1946: Marriage of daughter Jewell Florene to Thurman Thomas Padgett on Saturday, 23 March in Teague, Texas
1951: John Irvin Tisdale enlisted U S army on 2 January
1952: Moved to Baytown, TX in the Fall; working as carpenter, Farnsworth & Chambers, building Baytown/LaPorte tunnel
1953: Marriage of daughter Treva LaNelle to Marshall Ray Mattingly on 26 October
1957: Marriage of John Irvin Tisdale to Bonnie (Price) Black on Friday 1 June at 7:00 pm
1959: Marriage of daughter JoAnn to Richard Donnell Marshall on 11 September at 2nd Baptist Church in Highlands, (Harris Co.), Texas
1960: (circa)Working Hannah Construction as a general superintendent
1963: (circa)Moved to Mexia, Texas
1977: Death of David on 25 June; buried Newhope Cemetery (Freestone Co.) in Texas

OCCUPATIONS:

Farnsworth & Chambers (carpenter)
J.A. Rains Construction (carpenter)
Hannah Construction (general superintendent)
Breaking Horses
Music For Dances (guitar)
Farmer Oil Fields
Cotton Gins
Swift & Co. (carpenter in cotton seed plant)
Carpenter
Construction
School Board (Shanks School)

QUESTIONS:

1. When did Harley Douglas marry?
2. Are dates on David Lloyd accurate, and how did he die?
3. Is there truly no birth certificate for Jewell Florene?

ACTION:

1. Obtain copies of all family held documents.
2. Contact Newhope Cemetery for information on David, wife Irene, son David Lloyd, mother Martha Eleanor, and any other family members who are interred there.
3. Contact Bureau of Vital Statistics for certificates which are unavailable locally.

Figure 7a: Sample Biographical Worksheet

Biographical Worksheet

Name

Year	Note

OCCUPATIONS:

QUESTIONS:

ACTION:

Item 7: Biographical Worksheet

Chapter 6

What Do I Do When It's Done?

Obviously this chapter only applies if you have made enough copies for other people. The card stock I bought for the cover came in a 250 count ream, but I didn't need 250 books. I made 100 copies instead, knowing I could always print more if I had so surprising a demand.

I chose to give one copy to each of my aunts, uncles and cousins. Had either of my grandparents been alive I would have given them a copy, and I would have given copies to anyone else who had submitted a story or stories. I also gave a copy to one of my best friends, who suffered through a year of me talking about little else, and one to a distant relative who is in charge of a family reunion. I did not learn of this relative or the family reunion until it was too late for the book. I chose to give her a copy and get on her mailing list so I could learn about reunions in the future. I also hoped she and others would send me stories for the next book. As the keeper of the Key family genealogy, she is also the one who blessed me with the extensive information I spoke of earlier. I had intended to give this book to my grandmother for Christmas, but she died before I could finish. Because of this, I did not charge for these copies. I gave them to her children instead.

I had a difficult decision to make when it came to charging. I did not want people to think my goal was to make a profit. I did have to cover mailing and copy costs, however, and needed to recoup some other expenses as well. I had known this book would cost me something, but I did not realize how each little item would add up. I think I finally calculated that I had invested around $60.00, plus untold hours, before I started mailing copies to my relatives. That $60.00 doesn't sound like much today, but at that time it was a lot of money to me.

Mailing costs varied some, depending on how many copies were going to the same address, but I averaged about $1.00 per book for envelopes and postage. I could have mailed everything book rate if I had really felt the need to save money. I chose to mail first class because it was important to me that the books arrive in good condition and quickly. Knowing I would be spending about $1.00 per copy to deliver any orders, I decided to charge $2.50 each. I might have charged more, but I really did feel it was more important to share the history with as many as possible than it was for me to make money. This is an issue you must decide for yourself.

After you mail the first copies you can either sit back and let the others hear about it through word of mouth, or you can spread the word through letters. Obviously, if you have a family reunion soon after, you can take them with you and more than likely return home empty-handed. You might also send a few sample copies to distant relatives. These sample copies you send might well lead to sales in other parts of the family.

I have a hard time with the word, "sales" because it gives the impression I was doing this for financial gain. On the other hand, I had to face the fact that I simply could not handle the expense of sending out an unpredictable number of books for free. It is also worth remembering that most people have little respect for things given freely. The expression "You get what you pay for" can sometimes work against you, I'm afraid.

To charge or not charge, to market the book or let it sell itself, these decisions are your own. But don't stop now that your book is complete. Remember why you began it in the first place — keep telling the tales.

Chapter 7

Last Words

I began this book, *Front Porch History,* after a friend suggested that such a book would give homeschoolers a unique tool. We in the homeschool community tend to emphasize the building of strong families and my friend pointed out that a family uniting to preserve its heritage would be taking great strides in this direction. It also doesn't hurt that it makes for a great homeschool project! You will find information on integrating family history and homeschooling in Appendix A.

I regret that it never occurred to me to involve my children in my first family book. While I began that book **for** my children, I never even thought about doing it **with** them. This shows how much the teacher had yet to learn, does it not? As I have said before, I strongly encourage you to get the entire family involved. Whatever your project, draw them all in according to their interests and abilities at the levels for which they are most suited. Children will be much more interested in the on-going process if a newsletter or book contains stories written about and/or by themselves, and most would jump at the opportunity to provide illustrations. My sons work with me now on our family newsletter and will play vital roles in our next family book. It will, as a result, be more genuinely a family book.

We've heard a lot in recent years about the failure of the family being a contributing factor to the United States' social problems. When I began this book, I did not connect it with the publicity being given the family. Only as time passed, and I became more sensitive to the issue myself, did I truly notice how much attention the family was getting. I heard it constantly from all sides; it seemed family had suddenly become a thing to be taken seriously.

The attention is good — I think. My only concern has been that the publicity would result in a fad that everyone would follow for a day, only to say sometime next week, "Well, we tried it and it didn't work." Family is not something you work on, like a car or a television, only when it isn't running properly. Family, to me, is more like a prized rose bush that requires proper nurturing to flourish. A rose that is planted and left to run wild can seem just fine. Yet the rose requires consistent care and attention to be its best.

I offer this book in hopes that you will put it and what it teaches to work for you and your family. Please don't lay it down, intending to start tomorrow and never getting a round "tuit" (around to it). Collecting and sharing the stories does not have to wait until you have all of your relatives' addresses, or until you purchase a computer, or until your youngest is a little older, or until you can take a vacation, or until... The most difficult part of any project is the beginning. Simply pick a place and start.

Appendix A

Family History and the Homeschool

by Peggy Flint

I can almost see some of you sitting there with a smile on your face. The thought of working together on a book about your family's history intrigues you and you eagerly start to make your plans. Then reality sets in. . .you stare at the mounds of laundry, the list of errands, and the still unfinished lesson plans. You reluctantly decide to do this at a later date — perhaps next summer — if you don't forget. Putting this book aside, you work on the laundry or dishes or school, possibly missing out on one of the greatest opportunities your family may ever have to work together.

You can create a book of your family's stories if you will integrate this into your school. It may mean that some other things will have less priority, for a season. You may decide to have 4 days per week of "traditional" school and work on your family's book on the fifth day. Perhaps you will even put formal subjects aside for a limited period of time while you focus on the stories you want to cherish. However you decide to do it, you can incorporate this project into your children's education. They will even gain some experience in some practical life skills! In fact, let's take a look at the skills they will need.

Your students will master many English skills as they work on this book with you. Brainstorm with them about sources for the stories, and then assist them in writing letters requesting information from your family. Help your children write interesting letters soliciting help from extended family members. Whether you receive the stories in letters, tapes, or personal interviews, you will want them edited for grammar and spelling. If the stories were shared on a tape, your students can even practice their typing skills as they transcribe the stories. I encourage you to edit one story with your children so they can see how to edit a story for grammar, punctuation and spelling. Once you have done that, let them take over the job of editing, perhaps at the rate of one story per day. You children may edit the stories on the computer, preparing them for a book. If so, work with them during the layout and design process but do not take that portion of the project away from them. Depending upon your word processing software they can add borders and clip art to the stories, along with changing the font styles and sizes.

Your children can also learn organization and research skills as they work on this book. They will need to decide how to organize the information they receive and may choose to set up folders to separate the tales by categories. For example, they may set up one folder for all the wedding stories and another for all the war stories. However, they may choose instead to design one folder per person and file the stories chronologically. Once again, if you are using this as a school project, I highly recommend that you allow your children to make those decisions.

Have your children work on a budget with you, sharing the financial decisions. Let them decide what type of paper they can afford and how they will mail the books. You will want to give some guidance and input, but your children also will want to have a say. They may appreciate the books more when they realize the cost in time, effort, and money.

If you or your students desire, you may want to study genealogy and design a family tree to put in your book. Using calligraphy for the names and dates would make this an attractive and informative addition. Your students might even design borders or copy a coat-of-arms for each of the family surnames.

Do not forget to involve your students in presenting these books to family members. They might include a short note with each book, thanking all of the contributors for their stories. In fact, they might want to autograph a copy and send it to the person who contributed THEIR favorite story. Don't be surprised if your children want to set a deadline for submissions for the next edition — one they want to do during their free time.

Some of you reading this book will want to do more than just create a book of family stories. You can see the benefits of integrating your family's stories with your schoolwork on a regular basis and would like to know how to integrate them into more subjects. In this case, I would suggest that you consider developing your own unit study around your family's history and traditional history topics.

Family History Unit Studies

For those who are wondering, a unit study is the process of taking one subject and focusing most of your academic endeavors on it. You can build unit studies around any subject to last for any length of time. As the creator of this unit study, you decide what to study, how to study it, what to emphasize, and how long you will take.

There are several advantages to unit studies. First of all, the whole family can work together on the same topic at the same time. Each member of the family contributes information and insight at their ability level. Each member may pick one portion of that topic to focus on. For example, a student who is very interested in wars can focus much of their research on wars their grandfather fought in while another student is learning about the fashions of their grandparents' days. When these insights are brought together and shared with the family, the whole family reaps the benefits of all the research done.

Another advantage to unit studies is that you pick the information that is meaningful to you. For example, if your family shares an interest in medicine, you decide how much attention to focus on that topic. Finally, there is a sense of unity when all members are studying the same subject. Not only do all members share the same studies, but your writing assignments, reading assignments, vocabulary words and craft projects can be designed around that topic. If you do some creative brainstorming, you can even bring in appropriate Scripture studies.

There are some drawbacks to unit studies, particularly homemade ones. Like baking a homemade cake, you will have to put forth some energy and effort to reach into your storehouse of knowledge and pull out the ingredients that will make the unit study successful. It will take an investment of your time as you research the subject and think of meaningful goals and activities. You will need to have a focus and keep on track so that the unit study has meaning for your family. You will want to feel confident that you are done when you actually complete your unit study, which means that you will need to have goals for the material you wish to cover. You will find, as you familiarize yourself with the layout of unit studies and brainstorm on the activities you can include, that planning your customized unit study can be "a piece of cake".

It is important to remember that every unit study is different, so there is no one list that will tell you what you MUST include. Also, while some units lend themselves well to certain activities, others do not. The items I try to include in my unit studies are: timeline work; vocabulary words; writing (one assignment per week);

oral reports; reading books, magazines and newspapers; dictation; hands-on experiences if appropriate; art, music and literature; Bible studies (of applicable verses); practical life application skills (cooking) and field trips. With each unit, I try to focus on one academic skill and one writing skill (perhaps learning how to alphabetize and write narrative stories). Having a list of activities to choose from is no benefit if you don't know how to plan a unit study, so let's look at that next.

Planning a unit study can be easy once you decide three things.

1. What do the students know already? What don't they know?
   If a student has already mastered the basic facts about World War II, it will frustrate them to go back and relearn them just because their grandfather fought overseas. However, the same student may be very interested in studying the types of weapons their grandfather used — or the places where he served.
2. How long do you want to spend on this unit study?
   Some people spend 3 weeks, others spend 4, and others spend 6-10 weeks on unit studies. Depending upon how much of your family history you know, you may want to spend a semester or even a full year on this study.
3. What do you need to cover in order for your students to be "done" with this study?
   Knowing this will help you to plan your main objectives and budget your time.

Using my own family history, let me demonstrate how I would integrate my family's history with academic subjects. For the sake of this demonstration, we will be studying World War II and investigating what my family members (specifically my and my husband's parents) were doing during the years of 1941-1945.

One of the first subjects I would consider is American and world history. Since my father served in the Army, I would have him share about the places he served overseas. My father-in-law also served in the Army and in the Army Air Corp (which later became the Air Force) and we would mark on a map the places where he was stationed during the war. Along with mapmaking, we would create a timeline of famous battles and where each of our fathers were during that battle. If our fathers met any famous people, we would mark that also.

Although the United States didn't grow geographically during this time, we can still study this subject. We would focus our geography studies on the areas where our fathers served during the war, studying how that location affected the war (Were there mountains that affected transportation, or a language barrier?). We could even do some cultural studies on those areas, to understand what our fathers experienced.

For science, we would consider what the medical techniques were like during this time period, or perhaps the weapons of war and how they changed over the course of the war. We could do an in-depth study of inventions, or, perhaps, we might research the principles behind the atomic bomb. We could study anything related to science or we could skip science completely and just focus on the historical studies of World War II.

Both my mother and mother-in-law stayed home during World War II and we could learn from them about the culture back here at home. Among the things I would be looking for are movie titles, popular music, art from that time period (posters would help to show us history too) and even the literature that was being printed. My mother was single and living away from home for 2 years, and she could share some of what her life was like as she wrote letters to the man who would become her husband. I have been told that The Waltons gives a fairly accurate picture of life during the war if you wanted to watch a television show.

Another area I would want to consider is hobbies. For example, during this time period many people grew vegetable gardens to assist in the war effort. Others used their musical talents to help relieve the stress the troops experienced. I would like to know what my relatives did with their free time during this era.

Some other topics we could study are economics, architecture and fashions. For example, my children have always been interested in the prices of things in the past. My mother often talks about how much you could do on very little money if you were creative, and even about the items they learned to do without. She has also shared about the styles of her day and what she thinks of them now.

Interview Questions

If you plan to tie family history into your study of history, be sure to prepare questions to ask your relatives. I was fascinated by my mother's answers to these questions:

- Where were you when you heard Pearl Harbor was bombed?
- What was your reaction?
- What was the first television show that you watched?
- What was the first movie you ever saw?
- Where were you when you heard that Kennedy was shot?

- How did you feel?
- How did you feel when you heard that WWII was over?
- Did you know anyone overseas?
- What did you do when they came home?

Look for events in history that your family experienced and be prepared to ask them about those times. It will certainly make history come alive!

It doesn't matter if you choose to study family history for the sake of learning more about your family, or to use it as a hook to interest your family in a unit study. The important thing is that you can use the study of your family history as a helpful addition to your homeschool if you plan things creatively. If you are really creative, you might even get caught up with the laundry too!

EDITOR'S NOTE: Peggy claims that you can get caught up with the laundry by having your KIDS do it while you read the stories out loud to them. We have yet to see it work — but it just might someday!

APPENDIX B:

Resources

The following resources (divided into rough categories) are a combination of items I have reviewed personally and those that have received good reviews elsewhere. While the addresses, phone numbers, and prices I provide here are current at the time of publication, they are subject to change. Regarding genealogy software, consider these few reviews a beginning only. Take the time to do your homework. Get current information from computer and genealogy magazines, and contact the companies with your questions.

Family Heritage

Celebration Lifeline: Family History Study Project
(family timeline kit)

Your family is history. I find myself saying this over and over again as I try to help others see their families in a new light. Just as history teachers know the value of depicting historical figures and events on a timeline, so does J&K Schooling see value in putting your own family's important happenings into a 'historical' perspective.

The *Celebration Lifeline* was created with family celebrations in mind. It contains fourteen 11"x17" cardstock timeline pages that cover the years 1900-1997 (Newer editions may continue through the current year). The upper section of each page is devoted to illustrations that signify events in American history. Below these illustrations is a dated timeline and plenty of space for you to add family photos, selections from the over 130 pre-drawn illustrations, and your own notes. All illustrations are hand-rendered line drawings. Color them to suit your tastes or, better yet, pass out the markers and let everyone in on the act.

The *Celebration Lifeline* kit also includes memory pages. The idea is to assemble the lifeline and display it at a party or family reunion. Encourage family members to use the memory pages to record their own experiences and thoughts as they view the timeline. After the party, place the memory pages on the back of the timeline sheets and take a trip to your local copy shop. You have permission to make as many copies as you like of the finished product, so you now have an heirloom to give over and over again. To make it truly lasting, you may wish to have it laminated. It is likely that the same business you choose for copies will laminate it for you, and perhaps even bind the pages into a book for a few dollars more.

Celebration Lifeline is $26 plus $4 shipping and handling. Order it from...

J&K Schooling
5350 Sunset Lane; Loretto, MN 55357
Ph: (612) 479-2286

Family History
(child's activity kit)

Family History is a Dorling Kindersley First Activity Pack designed for ages five and up. Like Dorling Kindersley's other activity packs, it is a box filled with fun. Open it and you first discover a seventeen-page activity book with projects that help you explore your family's history. Photos are the first topic of discussion. You find tips on 'reading' old photos and instructions for making your own photo album (but please use archival materials instead of the recommended common tissue and cardboard). Following pages discuss interviewing, gathering and displaying family treasures (even common items become treasures over time), your family tree, family names, coats of arms, personal seals, inventions, fashions, and toys. It concludes with suggestions for making a time capsule. This book reflects the typical Dorling Kindersley style, offering eye-pleasing pages with intriguing photos and fascinating bits of information.

Next in the box is the Family History Record Book. Like the activity book, it is 91/2" x 91/2", but its eleven pages are composed of line drawings waiting to be colored. This book offers creative, child-pleasing ways to record family history. It also teaches photography basics (the kit contains a pocket camera), provides space to mount a few pictures, and even has puzzles to tease the active mind.

Your box isn't empty yet. It still holds a 23" x 16" four-color family tree poster waiting for your own information and photographs. A small timeline runs along the bottom and you have a sheet of stickers to help you complete it. Finally, you have 24 cards for a game in which you pair up inventions, toys, and other items from the past and present.

The *Family History Activity Pack* is $14.25 plus $3.50 shipping and handling. Order it from...

The Learning Home Educational Materials
5573 Ashbourne Road
Baltimore MD 21227-2813
Ph: (410) 536-5990
Email: learnghome@aol.com
Web: http://members.aol.com/learnghome

Gift of Heritage
(how-to video)

If you intend to create your own family heritage video, interweaving photos, records, old movies, and interviews, get your hands on *Gift of Heritage*. In this 60 minute instructional video, Mary Lou Peterson carefully guides you through the steps required to produce a professional quality video record of your family's history.

Peterson leaves nothing out. She begins by offering suggestions for gathering, preserving, and organizing family records and resources (photos, etc.). She then discusses your video, suggesting segments you may wish to include before she continues through the steps of video production. She covers details the novice may not think of, such as the effectiveness of using background music, sound effects, pictures and maps from the time period being discussed. She introduces the technical aspects of professional quality video production and gives clear, detailed explanations of the organizational tools and tricks she found most helpful. She gives excellent production tips, warns of potential pitfalls, and offers many options for each phase of the process. At the end, she even introduces a representative of a professional production company. He reiterates some of the things Peterson has already told you and gives a potpourri of professional advice, with demonstrations showing why you should do some things in specific ways.

Mary Lou Peterson doesn't just tell you; she shows you. Gift of Heritage abounds with practical help and illustrative clips from her own family video. Seeing what she created for her family inspires you to do the same for yours and, while she doesn't downplay the work required, she leaves you knowing it can be done.

Gift of Heritage is $29.95 plus $4 shipping and handling. The author has offered a discount to those who mention this book when they order, so you may wish to call first to confirm the price. Order it from...

Mary Lou Productions
P.O. Box 17233; Minneapolis, MN 55417
Ph: (800) 774-8511 or (612) 726-9432 Fax: (612) 727-2705
Web: http://www.giftofheritage.com

The Grandparents Video Interview Kit
(interview kit)

Videotaped interviews are our best option when we want to capture for our children the unique persons that are their grandparents. In a 60-90 minute video you can record for posterity little-known details about your parents' lives. You can create a living picture of who they are today. You can offer your parents the opportunity to give of themselves to future generations. *The Grandparents Video Interview Kit* offers the guidance you need to do it right.

The kit comes to you as three color-coded packets in a protective folder. The first packet contains complete instructions in the form of books and a letter. The Producer's Handbook goes to the person who will be responsible for the entire project. The *Camera Person's Guide* gives the camera operator in-depth tips. The *Interviewer's Guidebook* takes the interviewer step-by-step through the interview process. (You could, by the way, be both producer and either camera person or interviewer.) Last in this packet is four copies of the *"To Our Dear Interviewee"* letter. This letter tells the grandparent everything he or she needs to know to be ready for the interview.

Next comes the *Script* packet. It contains a copy of the interview script, which is designed to obtain the most comprehensive interview possible in 60-90 minutes. It also holds four introduction forms, four interviewee profile forms, and a news highlights form. You complete these three forms prior to each session and insert them into the script.

Finally, the *Accessories* packet holds registration and comment cards, four pages of pre-printed videocassette labels, eight video diary cards, coupons, and order forms. StarMark carries other products, including professional quality video tapes and other video interview kits (*Child's Annual, Parent's,* and *Pre-Wedding* are all available as of this printing).

This kit leaves nothing to chance. The books explain all steps clearly and simply, telling you exactly how to select the right equipment, arrange your set and lighting for the interview, stop and start recording... everything. The kit also contains sufficient printed materials (letters, labels, etc.) to complete four video taped conversations. Perhaps best of all, the method used requires no editing. Even a video novice could produce excellent results using the guidelines given here.

The *Grandparents Video Interview Kit* is $29.95 plus $4 shipping and handling. Order it from...

StarMark Family Group
P.O. Box 5116; Borger, TX 79008-5116
Ph: (800) 346-3830 or (806) 273-3830
Email: starmark@arn.net

Legacy
(family history workbook)

Legacy is a 208 page workbook that begins with your child's birth and works backwards through your family's history. The book's layout is simple; pages contain questions and blocks of space in which you (or the pertinent parties) write the answers.

Chapters 1 through 15 deal with personalized information about your child and each level of his ancestors through the second great-grandparents and beyond. The questions in these chapters help you discover the interesting and exciting details of family members' lives as well as pertinent facts about the days they live(d) in.

Some things you will cover are...

- Full Name - significance of name or who the person was named after
- Current events at time of birth
- Descriptions of siblings, their characteristics, and special memories
- A typical day at home - what it was like
- Popular styles while the person was growing up (clothes, hair, music, etc.)
- Some of the person's dreams - work, life, marriage, children
- Medical history of the family
- Wars that occurred during the person's lifetime and wars he or she served in
- "I'll never forget the time. . ."
- Marriage and child raising advice

The 'questions' (few are actually worded as questions) are varied and comprehensive. This would make an excellent guideline for family interviews and the questions it offers could inspire family stories. Pages in the back of the book allow you to add photos and additional information.

Because this book is consumable, you would need one book for each child. I advise against mounting actual photos in the back, but copying photos and mounting the copies would be an excellent option. Even if you prefer to present your family history in some other manner, this is still an excellent source for interview questions and story starters. It suggests topics of conversation that you may not think of otherwise.

Legacy is $18 plus $2 shipping and handling. Order it from...

Cheryl Pryor
Higher Priority Publishing
5304 Kingswood Dr.; Orlando FL 32810

Genealogy — General

Do People Grow on Family Trees? Genealogy for Kids and Other Beginners
(how-to book)

Ira Wolfman's 178 page paperback book is an excellent introduction for both children and adults. Written in a comfortable, conversational style, it abounds not only with the basics of genealogy but with photos, accounts of exciting 'finds,' pages of fascinating extra bits of information, tips on sharing your family history, and one of the most thorough explanations of immigration I've ever seen.

Step-by-step instructions lead you through the basics of genealogy, record keeping, and preservation. Interesting side notes explain such things as how to interpret old styles of handwriting, tracing your ancestors across the ocean, and what happened when we switched from the Julian to the Gregorian calendar in 1752 (we 'lost' 12 days). The book includes interview tips, shares some creative ways others have chosen to display their family trees, has pages of advice on planning a family reunion, and gives accounts of others' successes that will inspire you in your own search. The appendix contains a collection of forms, charts, addresses and more.

Homeschoolers should take advantage of this book's information to do a mini-study on immigration. Wolfman covers every aspect from why people left their homelands through the processes they followed on arrival and the special challenges that awaited them in this new country called America. Tales of individual immigrants' experiences keep these chapters lively and entertaining. Truly, the entire book is one interesting page after another.

Do People Grow on Family Trees? (ISBN: 0-89480-348-4) is published by Workman Publishing and sells for $9.95 in bookstores.

Everton Publishers, Inc.
(books, magazines, software)

Everton is a name to remember. Two of the most notable things this publishing company offers are The Handy Book for Genealogists and *Everton's Genealogical Helper.*

As this book goes to print, The Handy Book for Genealogists is being revised. The revision will be in high demand by professionals and hobbyists alike. It offers invaluable information about each of the states and all of the counties that ever existed in them.

This book makes tracking down those elusive records much easier. The 9th edition should be available soon and you should find previous editions in your local library.

Everton's Genealogical Helper is a bi-monthly magazine (current rates $24.00 per year US, $26.10 per year foreign) that is published specifically to put family historians in touch with one another. You can browse the ads to find researchers who are climbing your family tree or place an ad of your own. Even the commercial advertisements are helpful, offering you information about services you might not learn about elsewhere.

Everton's *Ancestor Research Tool*, a genealogy program, is also reviewed separately in this appendix.

The Everton Publishers, Inc.
P O Box 368; Logan, Utah 84323-0368
Ph: (800) 443-6325 Fax: (801) 752-0425
Web: http://www.everton.com

Family History Centers

Coordinating their efforts with the *Family History Library* in Salt Lake City, Utah, local *Family History Centers* make vast amounts of genealogical information available to any who come take advantage of their services. To find a center near you, either contact a local LDS congregation, preferably on a Sunday, or call the following 800 number.

Ph: (800) 346-6044

Family History Library
(library)

The *Family History Library* of the Church of Jesus Christ of Latter-day Saints is the largest genealogy library. Most of their records date from about 1550-1910 and include listings from around the world. You can write them for a list of the services they provide as well as information about their local *Family History Centers*.

Family History Library
35 North West Temple Street
Salt Lake City, Utah 84150

Genealogy Online
(how-to book)

Elizabeth Powell Crowe has accomplished the daunting task of writing a guide to the genealogy online world, and has done as excellent job of it. While the online world is constantly growing and changing, this book contains such information that it will remain valid for a very long time.

In 372 pages, Crowe details the hardware and software you need to access both local and Internet services. She also explains local Bulletin Board Services (BBS's), USENET Newsgroups, mailing lists, the World Wide Web and search engines. She discusses online services such as America Online and Prodigy, and tells of publishers' offerings. She also devotes chapters to the Church of Jesus Christ of Latter-Day Saints, Online Library Card Catalogs, and the Library of Congress Online. Those who take genealogy seriously and understand the potential of online research will want to take a look at this one.

Genealogy Online is published by McGraw Hill and sells for $24.95 in bookstores.

National Archives & Records Administration

The *National Archives & Records Administration* is the agency responsible for overseeing the management of the federal government's records. They offer brochures which explain how to access these records.

National Archives & Records Administration
Washington, DC 20408
Web: http://www.nara.gov/

National Genealogical Society

The National Genealogical Society (NGS) is the leading genealogical society in America. Membership brings you conference discounts, *The National Genealogical Society Quarterly*, the bi-monthly *National Genealogical Society Newsletter*, and the Computer Interest Group Digest (also bi-monthly). Members also have access to the NGS Library (which also loans volumes by mail), NGS educational courses, networking, a series of special publications, and more.

Individual memberships are $40. Family memberships are $50. Student membership is $25 (student ID required). There are also life, benefactor, sustaining, contributing, and institutional memberships available.

National Genealogical Society
4527 17th Street North; Arlington, Virginia 22207-2399
Ph: (800) 473-0060 Fax: (703)525-0052?
Email: ngs@ngsgenealogy.org
Web: http://www.ngsgenealogy.org/

Rootstamps™
(rubber stamps)

What would we do without the fun stuff? Collecting and sharing the stories, and tracking down elusive ancestors is already fun, but the extras make it more so. *Rootstamps*™ offers extras in the form of deeply etched rubber stamps, stamp pads, embossing powders, parchment papers, decorative scissors, paper punches, and much more. They have designs to please everyone, but their specialty is genealogy and family heritage. Nearly a thousand stamp designs in a wide variety of styles offer something to satisfy the most particular stamper, and the catalog even suggests creative ways to use the stamps.

Stamps range in price from $5 to $7.50. *Rootstamps*™ will also sell the stamps unmounted (either rubber only, or rubber and cushion) at a substantial discount. Unmounted stamps receive a reduced shipping charge. They carry more decorative scissors and paper punches than I have ever seen in one catalog. Punches range from $6 to $10. My favorites are the corner punches. These decorate the corners of your paper with an attractive edge and complementary cut-out.

The *Rootstamps*™ catalog is $2, which is refundable with your first order. Send $2 to...
Rootstamps
6479 White Pine Drive, Route 4 Box 1936; Lakeside, AZ 85929-9431
Email: roots@whitemtns.com
Web: http://www.whitemtns.com/~roots/

Genealogy — Software

Ancestor Research Tool
(software)

Ancestor Research Tool (ART) is as easy to use as they come. It opens directly to your family tree chart (pedigree) and from here you can move to and edit all of your records. The interface is typical Windows™, with a task bar offering the options of file, edit, add, search, reports, options, and quit. Buttons in the tree itself allow you to move to previous and next records and find, add, and edit records. Clicking on any person in the tree moves that person to the number one position where you can enter and edit their detailed data as well as making notes on the notepad. Trust me, there is nothing difficult about this program.

With ART you have the ability to print family group sheets, pedigree charts, descendant charts, ahnentafels (ancestor charts), and individual summaries. Pedigree charts and family group records go straight to the printer; all other charts may be previewed before printing. One small, but nice touch, is that all printouts contain your name, address, and phone number. This can be an invaluable asset when you begin trading information with other family members.

Ancestor Research Tool — Software Specs: Windows™ 3.1, 4MB RAM, 386 Processor (or better), 1.7MB free hard disk space

ART is shareware, with a registration fee of only $15. Order it from...

Everton Publishers, Inc.
P.O. Box 368; Logan, UT 84323-0368
Ph: (800) 443-6325
Email: order@everton.com
Web: http://www.everton.com/

Ancestry.com Inc.
(magazines, books, software)

Ancestry is a terrific resource for magazines, books, software and more.

Ancestry.com, Inc.
P.O. Box 990; Orem, UT 84059-0990
Ph: (800) ANCESTRY (262-3787)Fax: (801) 426-3501
Email: sales@ancestry-inc.com
web: http://www.ancestry.com

Family Matters
(software)

Family Matters® is a user-friendly shareware program designed to make tracking your family a pleasurable task. Like other Windows™ compatible programs, it uses a variety of icons to make entering data easier (it even has my personal favorite, the undo button). Your file opens directly to the last family group form you were working on, allowing you to pick up where you left off. All other functions are available while you work here, and moving between families and individuals is easy. You may customize your records to reflect specialized information, and can even insert pictures. You can enter an unlimited number of spouses, children, individuals, marriages, and inter-relationships as well as unlimited events. You also have large note pads for free-form text entry for both families and individuals.

Family Matters® lets you preview and print family trees, descendancy charts, individual and family group reports and four types of lists - individual, family, event and to do. The event list is especially interesting to the genealogist who wishes to view his family's heritage in the context of history. With its multiple ways of sorting information, you can create a chronological listing of events that makes adding your family to your homeschool timeline a cinch. With *Family Matters®* you can also create your own genealogical web pages, which would be not only fun, but educational as well.

Family Matters® will run under any version of Windows™. A version designed specifically for Windows™ 95/98 will be available by the time of this book's publication.

It sells for $25 plus $5 shipping, or you may download from the web and save shipping costs. Order from...

MatterWare
3522 Sandy Ridge Trail; DeLand, FL 32724
Ph: (904) 736-8030
Email: MatterWare@aol.com
Web: http://hometown.aol.com/matterware/index.html

Family Tree Maker
(software)

Family Tree Maker™ is one of the highest rated genealogy programs on the market. It is user-friendly, allowing you to jump right into transferring that hard-won information to your computer.

There are multiple versions of *Family Tree Maker*™. Whatever you want, one or more of these programs is bound to offer it. Sort and store information of all kinds, including video and audio clips. Print a wide variety of family trees and reports. Create multimedia family albums. Start your search for ancestral information in the *Family Finder Index*, which lists more than 170 million people. Create professional quality family books right in your own home. Access an unbelievable wealth of information and support through the *Family Tree Maker*™ website... Indeed, it would almost be easier to say what the software does not offer than to list all that it does.

Software Specs: Microsoft® Windows95™ or Windows98™ required; 486 or faster; 8 MB RAM (16 MB recommended); minimum 20 MB free hard disk space; 2X CD-ROM drive or faster; 640x480 display, and 16 colors or higher. *Family Tree Maker*®, depending on the version you choose, sells for anywhere from $29.99 to $89.99. *Family Tree Maker*® is also available for Power Macintosh. Contact...

Broderbund Software; Banner Blue Division
P.O. Box 100; Hiawatha, IA 52233-0100
Ph: (800) 548-1806 Fax: (319) 395-7449
Web: http://www.familytreemaker.com/

Ultimate Family Tree Platinum (software)

If you're serious about genealogy and want a professional level program that does everything but track your ancestors down for you, *Ultimate Family Tree*™ *Platinum* comes pretty darned close. I cannot possibly tell you everything this program does; the list would be too long and there would still be important elements missing. Its reports, customization options, web-based benefits, publication capabilities, tutorials, information access and more make it my favorite.

Rather than go into details about *Ultimate Family Tree*™ *Platinum's* capabilities, I will say that I have followed this software through several generations (from Roots IV™, through Roots V™, then the merger between two different programs that resulted in *Ultimate Family Tree*™ *Premier*, and now *Ultimate Family Tree*™ *Platinum*) and I have always been impressed.

Software Specs: Windows™ 3.1/Windows™ 95/98 Compatible, 486DX/66 MHz or greater, color VGA monitor 256 colors minimum thousands of colors capable video card recommended when using color photographs, double-speed CD-ROM drive and sound card. Windows™ 95/98 Systems: 16MB RAM min, 70 MB hard disk space.

Windows™ 3.1 Systems: 8 MB RAM min, 49 MB of hard disk space. PictureWorks Technology NetCard(tm) requires Windows™ 95, and email software that accepts file attachments. E-mail software is not included. Optional: scanner, modem (14.4K bps or faster recommended).

Ultimate Family Tree™ Platinum sells for $69.95.

Palladium Interactive
899 Northgate Drive, Fourth Floor; San Rafael, CA 94903
Ph: (415) 446-1700 Fax: (415) 446-1730
Email: webstar@palladium.net
Web: http://www.uftree.com/

Miscellaneous

Creating Books With Children
(how-to book)

Valerie Bendt designed this book for use as a guide to a six week book-making unit. This obviously means it is geared to homeschooling families, but anyone interested in producing high quality hardbound books (family books, for instance) will appreciate it as a fabulous resource.

Week one begins with prewriting activities. In Week two you write the stories. Week three covers text layout and editing. Week four is set aside for illustrating your story. You develop the beginning and ending pages and book jacket in week five and assemble the book in week six.

Bendt gives detailed, illustrated directions for each step, guiding you through the process in such a manner that the potentially intimidating task of creating a hardbound book is made simple. Her books are of a specific size (81/2" by 11" with 17 pages) but the skills apply to any hardbound book. As I've said before, Creating Books With Children would be of value to homeschoolers and non-homeschoolers alike.

Creating Books With Children sells for around $18. For more information, contact the publisher...

Common Sense Press
P.O. Box 1365; 8786 Highway 21; Melrose FL 32666

Available from:
Greenleaf Press
3761 Highway 109 N., Unit D; Lebanon, TN 37087
Ph: (800) 311-1508 (orders) or (615) 449-1617
Email: greenleafpress@softek.net
Web: http://www.greenleafpress.com

Creative Memories®
(photo preservation / scrapbooking supplies)

Creative Memories® has representatives around the country who will come into your home and hold classes on storing your photographs in delightful, photo-safe ways. Then, once you've begun scrapbooking (as it's called), they can offer you all the support you need by way of personal input and availability of supplies. Be careful; these people are known for creating scrapbook addicts (I'm glad to say I am one). Creative Memories® sells not only photo-safe albums and mounting supplies, but also creative items such as cropping supplies, templates, stickers, acid-free papers, and photo-safe pens. Call them for the name of a representative near you.

Creative Memories
Box 1839; St. Cloud, MN 56302-1839
Ph: (800) 341-5275
Web: http://www.creativememories.com/

DOTS™ & Close to My Heart™
(photo preservation/scrapbooking & stamping supplies)

DOTS™ is a rubber stamp company that has jumped into the scrapbooking field with both feet. *Close to My Heart™* is their scrapbooking line and through it they offer beautiful albums and a wide assortment of supplies. All of their materials are of high quality and their papers are some of the most popular available. There is a charge for their superb catalog/idea book, but it is well worth the investment. You can also earn your book free by having a *DOTS™* representative hold a party in your home. Call the *DOTS™* referral line for the number of a representative near you.
Ph: (888) 655-6552

How to Create Your Own Unit Study
(how-to book)

Feeling that family heritage is an ideal topic for a unit study and wanting to encourage you to use it as such, I knew I had to include this book in the appendix. Homeschoolers consider Valerie Bendt an expert when it comes to unit studies, and she shares her expertise here. This book is a boon to those who are interested in unit studies but don't know where to start.

Bendt begins with a discussion of educational philosophies and curriculum. She talks about what unit studies are and what they are not, and introduces the basics of how she plans and implements her own family's units. The book's pages take you step by step through the planning process. Bendt suggests possible resources and tips on keeping your unit costs low. She discusses different areas of study (traditional school subjects) and ways to introduce each into your units. She gives you nuts and bolts advice on the details and even shares her record keeping system. At the end, she includes sample units, descriptions of various reference books, and a list of resource addresses. If you are at all interested in the unit study approach to education, get your hands on this book.

How to Create Your Own Unit Study sells for around $16. For more information, contact the publisher at...

Common Sense Press
P.O. Box 1365; 8786 Highway 21; Melrose FL 32666

Available from:
Greenleaf Press
3761 Highway 109 N., Unit D; Lebanon, TN 37087
Ph: (800) 311-1508 (orders) or (615) 449-1617
Email: greenleafpress@softek.net
Web: http://www.greenleafpress.com

Make Your Own Book
(complete book making kit)

Running Press produces some of the most creatively entertaining educational kits on the market and Make Your Own Book is no exception. Within this one box you find virtually everything you need (including a cover and paste) to create a 32 page, hand-bound, hardback book, but this is not all you find.

The Bookmaking Handbook not only shares the how-to's of bookmaking, but the where-from's as well. It begins with a brief history of the written word, touching on the development and use of papyrus, clay, silk, and parchment and the several forms of fiber paper that man has used through time. It then discusses the history of printing from the use of wood blocks, developed in China in 770 AD to today's computer driven presses. It gives an in-depth account of the history of bookbinding before proceeding to an explanation of writing types (with various examples of both fiction and non-fiction). It ends with step-by-step instructions for creating your own books from first idea to finished product.

While you study the intriguing history of the book (children won't know it's 'study'), you can follow the book's directions and make your own paper or experiment with potato printing. Your finished book is the end result of days or weeks spent in fascinating pursuit. Homeschoolers, this kit would be a great foundation for a mini-unit or excellent enrichment material for any curriculum.

The Make Your Own Book Kit is $18.95 plus $4 shipping and handling. Order it from...

In His Steps
1618 Kendolph; Denton, Texas 76205
Ph: (940) 566-6123 or (800) 583-1336 (orders only)
Email: inhissteps@juno.com
Web: http://www.inhissteps.com

My Time
(archival materials)

Preserving your precious family history items is serious business and you want the best archive quality materials to help you take care of them. *My Time* is an excellent resource. Their catalog goes beyond the storage of photographs and into document and even clothing protection. They sell such items as... photo/negative boxes and envelopes; photo sleeves; cotton gloves; albums and assorted album pages;

mounting products; document boxes, folders and sleeves; acid free bond paper, oversized folders and storage boxes; encapsulation materials; garment/quilt preservation materials; and pens. *My Time* also sells books that teach preservation how-to's. While there are larger archival materials companies out there, the more professional catalogs can be so big they leave you overwhelmed. *My Time* is an excellent place to start, offering the materials you will need in a catalog filled with much encouragement and many helpful hints.

My Time
P.O. Box 8247; Warwick, RI 02888
Ph: (401)941-1073
Web: http://www.mytime.com

APPENDIX C:

Forms & Worksheets

YOU
1
Name: ____________
Place: ____________
Born: ____________
Place: ____________
Married: ____________
Place: ____________
Died: ____________
Place: ____________

SPOUSE (of No.1)
Name ____________

FATHER (OF NO.1)
2
Name: ____________
Born: ____________
Place: ____________
Married: ____________
Place: ____________
Died: ____________

MOTHER (OF NO.1)
3
Name: ____________
Born: ____________
Place: ____________
Died: ____________
Place: ____________

FATHER (OF NO.2)
4
Name: ____________
Born: ____________
Place: ____________
Married: ____________
Place: ____________
Died: ____________
Place: ____________

MOTHER (OF NO.2)
5
Name: ____________
Born: ____________
Place: ____________
Died: ____________
Place: ____________

FATHER (OF NO.3)
6
Name: ____________
Born: ____________
Place: ____________
Married: ____________
Place: ____________
Died: ____________
Place: ____________

MOTHER (OF NO.3)
7
Name: ____________
Born: ____________
Place: ____________
Died: ____________
Place: ____________

(FATHER OF NO.4)
8
Name: ____________
Born: ____________
Place: ____________
Married: ____________
Place: ____________
Died: ____________

MOTHER (OF NO.4)
9
Name: ____________
Born: ____________
Place: ____________
Died: ____________

FATHER (OF NO.5)
10
Name: ____________
Born: ____________
Place: ____________
Married: ____________
Place: ____________
Died: ____________

MOTHER (OF NO.5)
11
Name: ____________
Born: ____________
Place: ____________
Died: ____________

FATHER (OF NO.6)
12
Name: ____________
Born: ____________
Place: ____________
Married: ____________
Place: ____________
Died: ____________

MOTHER (OF NO.6)
13
Name: ____________
Born: ____________
Place: ____________
Died: ____________

FATHER (OF NO.7)
14
Name: ____________
Born: ____________
Place: ____________
Married: ____________
Place: ____________
Died: ____________

Mother (of no.7)
15
Name: ____________
Born: ____________
Place: ____________
Died: ____________

Figure 5: Family Tree (or Pedigree).

Family Group Sheet

Date: ______________________________

HUSBAND: ______________________________

BORN: ______________________________

MARRIED: ______________________________

DIED: ______________________________

BURIED: ______________________________

FATHER: ______________________________

MOTHER: ______________________________

WIFE: ______________________________

BORN: ______________________________

DIED: ______________________________

BURIED: ______________________________

FATHER: ______________________________

MOTHER: ______________________________

CHILDREN

1. NAME: ______________________________ (M/F)

BORN: ______________________________

MARRIED: ______________________________

DIED: ______________________________

BURIED: ______________________________

2. NAME: ______________________________ (M/F)

BORN: ______________________________

MARRIED: ______________________________

DIED: ______________________________

BURIED: ______________________________

3. NAME: ______________________________ (M/F)

BORN: ______________________________

MARRIED: ______________________________

DIED: ______________________________

BURIED: ______________________________

Figure 6: Family Group Worksheet

4. NAME: ______________________________ (M/F) __________

BORN: ______________________________

MARRIED: ______________________________

DIED: ______________________________

BURIED: ______________________________

5. NAME: ______________________________ (M/F) __________

BORN: ______________________________

MARRIED: ______________________________

DIED: ______________________________

BURIED: ______________________________

6. NAME: ______________________________ (M/F) __________

BORN: ______________________________

MARRIED: ______________________________

DIED: ______________________________

BURIED: ______________________________

7. NAME: ______________________________ (M/F) __________

BORN: ______________________________

MARRIED: ______________________________

DIED: ______________________________

BURIED: ______________________________

8. NAME: ______________________________ (M/F) __________

BORN: ______________________________

MARRIED: ______________________________

DIED: ______________________________

BURIED: ______________________________

9. NAME: ______________________________ (M/F) __________

BORN: ______________________________

MARRIED: ______________________________

DIED: ______________________________

BURIED: ______________________________

Figure 6: Family Group Worksheet

Biographical Worksheet

Name

Year	Note

OCCUPATIONS:

QUESTIONS:

ACTION:

Item 7: Biographical Worksheet